DATE DUE

DEMCO

HINDU AND SIKH
FAITHS in AMERICA

GAIL M. HARLEY

J. GORDON MELTON, SERIES EDITOR

Facts On File, Inc.

HINDU AND SIKH FAITHS IN AMERICA
Faith in America

Facts On File, Inc.
132 West 31st Street
New York NY 10001

Library of Congress Cataloging-in-Publication Data

Harley, Gail M.
   Hindu and Sikh faiths in America / Gail M. Harley.
    p. cm — (Faith in America)
   Includes bibliographical references and index.
   ISBN 0-8160-4987-4
    1. Hinduism—United States—History. 2. Sikhism—United States—History. 3. Asian Americans—Religious life—United States. 4. India—Religion. I. Series.

   BL1108.7.U6 H36 2002
   294.5'0973—dc21   2002034740

Facts On File books are available at special discounts when purchased in bulk quantities for businesses, associations, institutions, or sales promotions. Please call our Special Sales Department in New York at (212) 967-8800 or (800) 322-8755.

You can find Facts On File on the World Wide Web at http://www.factsonfile.com

Produced by the Shoreline Publishing Group LLC
Editorial Director: James Buckley Jr.
Contributing Editor: Beth Adelman
Designed by Thomas Carling, Carling Design, Inc.
Index by Nanette Cardon, IRIS

Photo credits:
Cover: AP/Wide World (3); Corbis (center right). AP/Wide World: 15, 32, 45, 46, 49, 55, 61, 77, 78, 89, 93; Courtesy BAPS: 83; Courtesy Chinmaya Mission West: 74; Courtesy Christian Science Association: 29; Corbis: 27, 42, 53; Digital Stock: 6, 56; Dinodia Photo Library: 13; Getty Images: 50, 64, 86; Courtesy Hindu Temple Society of North America: 70, 96; Courtesy Ma Jaya River School: 91; Courtesy D.S. Singh family 81; Courtesy Ravpreet Singh: 21, 99; Courtesy Vedanta Society: 9, 10, 11, 26; Vancouver Public Library 31, 36.

Printed in the United States of America

VB 10 9 8 7 6 5 4 3 2 1

This book is printed on acid-free paper.

CONTENTS

FOREWORD

AMERICA BEGINS A NEW MILLENNIUM AS ONE OF THE MOST RELIGIOUSLY diverse nations of all time. Nowhere else in the world do so many people—offered a choice free from government influence—identify with such a wide range of religious and spiritual communities. Nowhere else has the human search for meaning been so varied. In America today, there are communities and centers for worship representing all of the world's religions.

The American landscape is dotted with churches, temples, synagogues, and mosques. Zen Buddhist zendos sit next to Pentecostal tabernacles. Hasidic Jews walk the streets with Hindu swamis. Most amazing of all, relatively little conflict has occurred among religions in America. This fact, combined with a high level of tolerance of one another's beliefs and practices, has let America produce people of goodwill ready to try to resolve any tensions that might emerge.

The Faith in America series celebrates America's diverse religious heritage. People of faith and ideals who longed for a better world have created a unique society where freedom of religious expression is a keynote of culture. The freedom that America offers to people of faith means that not only have ancient religions found a home here, but that newer forms of expressing spirituality have also taken root. From huge churches in large cities to small spiritual communities in towns and villages, faith in America has never been stronger. The paths that different religions have taken through American history is just one of the stories readers will find in this series.

Like anything people create, religion is far from perfect. However, its contribution to the culture and its ability to help people are impressive, and these accomplishments will be found in all the books in the series. Meanwhile, awareness and tolerance of the different paths our neighbors take to the spiritual life has become an increasingly important part of citizenship in America.

Today, more than ever, America as a whole puts its faith in freedom—the freedom to believe.

Hindu and Sikh Faiths in America

The Indian subcontinent was the birthplace of what would come to be known as Hinduism and Sikhism after European settlers entered the region and tried to make sense of the confusing array of spiritual pathways opened to them. The initial attitudes of these Europeans were negative. Those raised in Western Christian backgrounds had trouble appreciating the depth of the very different spiritual life Hindus presented. Over the centuries, however, initial hostility to Hindu beliefs gave way to understanding and admiration of the spirituality and wisdom of Hindu traditions.

The transfer of Hinduism and Sikhism to America began late in the 19th century when the first gurus, or teachers, arrived. However, before a real community could emerge, the Indian American community was caught in the net of anti-Asian discriminatory legislation passed early in the 20th century. Only with repeal of the Asian Exclusion Act in 1965 was Hinduism and Sikhism given the opportunity to participate in the free flow of religious ideas and practice in American society.

The steady growth of the Hindu and Sikh communities has followed two paths since the mid-'60s. First, Indians have moved to the United States and tried to recreate their life at home through numerous Asian-American associations, usually around traditional temples, several hundred of which can now be found in every part of the United States. Second, young adults flocked to sit at the feet of gurus who offered various forms of Hindu wisdom to a new generation of spiritual seekers. Many Americans were just as confused about the Indian teachers as Europeans in India had been early in the 19th century. Hindu leaders endured a period of controversy before being able to take their place at the banquet table of America's faith. *Hindu and Sikh Faiths in America* opens up the exotic world of Hindu and Sikh life and tells the story of these faiths in the United States, a story that is still in its initial stages.

— *J. Gordon Melton, Series Editor*

INTRODUCTION

Hindu and Sikh Origins and Beliefs

HINDUISM IS ONE OF THE LARGEST AND MOST COMPLEX RELIGIONS IN the world. While most Hindus live in India, which is the home of Hinduism as a religion, there are a growing number of Hindus and American converts to Hindu religious movements in America. As will be seen, Hinduism has many basic beliefs, but also many different ways of expressing them and practicing them.

Sikhs, too, mostly come from India. Their religion was founded by a spiritual leader named Guru Nanak in the early 16th century in India. Sikhism is related to Hinduism and was influenced by Islam. Many immigrants from the northern areas of India, primarily a region called the Punjab, now live in Sikh communities found throughout the United States.

Americans and peoples from other countries who have never lived in India have also chosen to embrace certain aspects of Hinduism, giving it a religious home far from the land of its birth. Hindu people outside of India are primarily found in the United States, Great Britain, Canada, Sri Lanka, Indonesia, Fiji, South Africa, Kenya, Pakistan, Bangladesh, and Trinidad.

In some countries, Hindus and Sikhs are a religious and ethnic minority. In the United States, for example, they total about 1.5 million people and make up a small percentage of all the residents of the country. However, they are a visible presence in schools, businesses, and the workplace.

Hindus Get a Name

Hinduism evolved gradually instead of being created at one time by a person or group. It does not have a specific founder such as Christianity had in Jesus and Islam had in Mohammad. Instead, Hinduism developed over time from many philosophies and religious ideas (sometimes contradicting each other). These traditions shaped many different forms of Hinduism.

The name Hindu comes from a mispronunciation of the river Sindhu in the northern part of India. The people of ancient Persia, which is now Iran, were India's neighbors to the west. They first mispronounced the Sindhu. The name came to mean the people who were not of the Islamic faith. Later, the Turks, Arabs, and Afghans all came to use the word Hindu to describe people who were not born into Islam. Of course, not everyone who dwelled in that geographical region was Hindu. Other names were later given to other ethnic groups and religions whose people lived in that area but did not practice Hinduism.

Hinduism was formed in its early stages by religious practices performed in the northwest of India around the Indus Valley. Indo-Europeans, or Aryans, who came from northern Europe driving two-man chariots, invaded the territory of the peaceful people now called Dravidians. These Aryans, who came in waves of migrations starting about 5,000 years ago, remained in India. They brought with them the language Sanskrit, for which no writing system had been developed yet. Another group of Aryans migrated to Europe and the British Isles (in fact, Ireland is named for them). The belief in sky gods the Aryans brought with them to India merged, over time, with the ancient goddesses and gods of the Dravidians. A festive and colorful tradition developed through the centuries and is today called Hinduism.

A Cultural Mosaic

Afghans, Turks, British, and other invaders helped shape the religious culture of India, creating a colorful blend of various religious traditions. From the earliest days that civilizations began to travel across Asia to explore and trade with each other, the lands of India were located on the major routes connecting Asia and Europe. Peoples from faraway lands traveled along these routes, each influencing the culture, language, and religion in India helping to make it the cultural mosaic it is today.

Many languages are spoken by Hindus, including English. Some languages spoken in India today are related to Sanskrit and others are from a family of languages spoken by the original people of India. These original people are believed by some to be the Tamils, who now live in southern India. Sanskrit is a legacy from the Aryans and is a major religious language. However, only scholars know how to read Sanskrit. Residents of specific regions in India also have their own regional languages.

Hindus in America may chant in Sanskrit while they are worshiping, but day to day conversation is mostly in English or Hindi, which are the main languages of India.

Shiva and his symbols
Surrounding the god Shiva in this traditional painting, provided by the Vedanta Society, are his many symbols: the trident (right), the serpent (on his right shoulder), and the flowing river.

A musical deity
Krishna is one of the most famous gods in the Hindu pantheon. He is depicted in many different ways in all kinds of art forms. This painting, also provided by the Vedanta Society, shows him playing a flute that delivers the melodies of love.

Hindu Gods and Goddesses

Hinduism is both polytheistic, meaning it has many gods and goddesses, and monistic, which means that God is One. To Hindus, Brahma is the Ultimate Reality or God. Hindu mythology tells of the exploits of gods and goddesses that have aspects of human and divine.

Many Hindu homes have beautiful artwork and carved statues depicting the family's favorite deities. The home altar is considered sacred space within the home, dedicated to the deity that the family has chosen. *Puja* is the daily devotion that honors their chosen God. During *puja*, the family offers prayers, burns fragrant incense, and decorates the sacred altar with flowers. They place a little rice on the altar to signify the blessings the family has received from their religious activity.

The Hindu gods and goddesses are noted for their many different attributes. Stories about them are colorful and dramatic and include positive and negative aspects of life. A number of gods and goddesses are known by many names and this is sometimes confusing. Here we will use the most well-known names for the gods and their consorts or companions. However you may read other books where another name is used.

Brahma is the creator god. He appears with four heads and hands and is seated upon a lotus flower. The lotus is very well-known in India, although it is not often found in America. Every hand of Brahma holds an article of importance: a tool, a water pot, a rosary, and books representing the Vedas (ancient Indian sacred writings; see page 14).

Vishnu, the preserver god, also has four hands. He holds a conch shell representing the divine sound "om" in one hand. In the others, he holds a round discus that symbolizes the preciousness of time, a lotus that means the glorious life, and a mace to show that life is about

Hero at the ready
The god Rama (center) is often pictured with his wife Sita, brother Lakshman, and devotee Hanuman, a monkey deity. Rama is the hero of the famous epic story the Ramayana. He is pictured with a bow and arrow, showing he is always ready to battle evil. This traditional painting was supplied by the Vedanta Society.

discipline as well as fun. Vishnu is usually portrayed with dark skin, a magical color. He sleeps upon the head of a coiled serpent who symbolizes the peace of a sleeping universe.

The god Shiva has several forms. Sometimes he is shown as a calm presence, other times his hair is wildly tangled. The sacred river Ganges is supposed to flow across his hair. He also holds a trident (a three-pronged pitchfork) with a serpent coiled around his neck and a crescent moon in his hands. Shiva denotes the victory over evil ideas and the harmony of human behavior. He often rides a bull named Nandi.

Krishna is one of the most worshiped gods in Hinduism. He is known for his bravery and the ability to destroy negative power. Sometimes he is shown playing a flute that delivers the melodies of love. His childhood sweetheart, Radha, is often shown with him, symbolizing eternal love. He is usually shown in paintings with blue or black skin.

These gods and goddesses, and others, have inconsistent stories and legends. Hindus are not very concerned with having the stories be exactly the same; their faith is not measured by facts. It is the interplay, the drama, the depictions of life that they relate to. When people speak about their favorite deity it is with reverence for the aspects of that god or goddess that show all the troubles that both humans and gods can get into.

Hindus also attend festivals and sacred services to honor other deities on holy occasions. At such festivals, young people dance and socialize. Young people who do not date are able to mingle with one another. The festivals are a time for community, for exchanging news and remembering ancient ways.

An important concept in Hinduism is that it is an inclusive religion. This means that Hinduism attempts to include everyone who wants to belong. Some other religions are exclusive. This means certain people who profess different beliefs about what is holy are kept out, and in some cases, maligned or treated disrespectfully.

Religious and Spiritual Writings

Hindu people love books and religious literature that tells about the exploits of their many gods and goddesses. Religious principles, spiritual teachings, history, and mythology are taught orally or through various forms of literature. Comic books have become popular ways to teach values, history, and religious precepts with tales of great adventure. Story books teach about the great heroes with colorful pictures so even children can enjoy the sagas of the gods and goddesses.

Hindus do not have a single book such as the New Testament for Christians, the Hebrew Bible for Jews, or the Qur'an for Muslims. A major Hindu spiritual book, however, is the Bhagavad Gita, which means "song of our lord." It is a book that many Hindus read over and over throughout their life.

Great leaders in India such as Mahatma Gandhi and Jawaharlal

A Most Famous Tale: The Bhagavad Gita

The Bhagavad Gita tells the story of a dilemma faced by Arjuna, a young warrior entangled in a family feud fought thousand of years ago in the foothills of the Himalayas. His wise chariot driver is the god Krishna in disguise (right, with beard). As they maneuver the chariot close to the battle lines, Arjuna sorrowfully laments that he is about to go into the war and perhaps kill his relatives fighting for the opposite side. Krishna advises him that it is his ethical and moral duty to fight. Krishna says to him "fight, Arjuna, but do not be attached to the spoils of war. Fight, Arjuna, but do not love killing. Fight, Arjuna, for you can kill the body in battle but you can not kill the soul."

The Gita teaches that the most important revelation for Arjuna is to know the intensity of his love for God (*bhakti*), to do his dharma (duty and responsibility), and know that his karma (actions) is clear with the fulfillment of his responsibility. All of these diverse paths will let him continue toward *moksa*, release from this world.

The most inspiring message from Krishna is that the soul is indestructible. The most practical idea is that deeds should be done because they need to be done and not out of attachment to them. The most divine teaching is that God alone gives the soul and only God can take it. The activities of mere mortals do not replace the single truth that God is all.

The Gita remains the most widely read book in Hinduism and is also well known by many people outside of the faith. Arjuna is one of the most popular heroes in religious literature.

Nehru read the Gita, as it is called for short, and were inspired by it. In the 1930s and 1940s, these men helped India proclaim her independence from the Great Britain. Gandhi also read the New Testament and was impressed with the Sermon on the Mount given by Jesus. Gandhi's belief about *ahimsa*, or nonviolence, as a method to gain equality later influenced Dr. Martin Luther King, Jr., who used peaceful nonviolence during the American Civil Rights movement in the 1960s.

While the Gita has been a classic text among Hindus, other sacred writings are equally important and a number of American-based Hindu religious movements organize their religious principles around other significant literature, as well.

Shruti Scripture

Hindu scripture, or sacred teachings, can be either *shruti*—that which is heard—or *smirti*—that which is remembered. Among the *shruti*, there are a number of holy books. The four Vedas are the oldest known literature, perhaps in the world, and are considered to be writings inspired by God. No one can say with certainty just how old the Vedas may be. However, some Vedic ideas pre-date the migration of the Aryans to India. They were chanted orally long before they were written down. They contain hymns and praises to God, priestly rituals, recipes for magic, and musical notes to be sung to the Holy. Among these notes is the chant of the sacred sound "om." The Vedas and the Upanishads (below) created the philosophical structure for other Hindu literature.

The Brahmanas were written after the Vedas and describe the important fire rituals. What may be the oldest recorded prayer in the world—the Gayatri—is chanted each day during the fire ritual to thank the sun for shining and ask for prosperity for everyone. Today, in the United States, burning candles often are used in ceremonies in place of large, holy fire pits.

The Upanishads are the latest *shruti* scripture. They show very creative thinking and a blossoming of curiosity by teachers and sages. Scholars think they were written down between 800 and 450 B.C.E. The word *upanishad* means to "sit near" a teacher, who is called in Sanskrit a guru. Most of the Upanishads are written in the form of dialogues between guru and *chela*. The *chela* is the student who receives private or oral spiritual teachings from the guru. A long time ago young men frequently went to live with their teachers in the forests away from the distractions of town life so they could study and learn as much as possible from the sages. These teachings concerned the relationship between humans and their souls (*atman*) and God (Brahma). Universal wisdoms were passed from guru to *chela* through each generation for more than 2,500 years. Young people still study these ancient writings and computers allow teachers and students real time interaction through the visual media.

The teachings in the Upanishads have become the hallmarks of Hindu thinking and philosophy. Many of the ideas and principles are reflected in the different forms of Hindu religions in America. A main feature of the Upanishads was to shift the religious focus from the fire ritual that we discussed earlier to personal involvement with the sacred through inquisitive thought. Sanskrit terms such as *mantra*, which means to repeat something, and karma which is the deed one does along

Sacred waters
Hindus consider many rivers or places where rivers merge to be sacred. Parts of the Ganges River in India (below) are regularly visited by faithful Hindus, who believe bathing in the water purifies them.

with the repercussions of it, have become familiar words among Americans. The Thirteen Principle Upanishads and books that teach only five or six of the Upanishads can be found in most city bookstores as modern people look to the older teachings for valuable truths about the human soul (*atman*) and God (Brahma). People in the new millennium are still interested about relationships that nourished humanity in the ancient divine quests. They continue to marvel about how all living beings were wedded to the cosmos through karma, their actions, and through *dharma*, the responsibility they took to do the right thing.

Smirti Texts

Smirti texts are considered to be less of divine origin than those of *shruti*. However, they are still significant. They include the great epic poem (probably the longest in the world) Mahabharata which has more than 90,000 stanzas. The stories found in the poem are available today in a film that takes 12 hours to show in its entirety. Despite its length it is shown by the Students of India Associations at most colleges and universities where Hindus matriculate. It is the story transmitted by the ancient sage and wise man Vyasa, who dictated it to the elephant-headed god of good fortune, Ganesha. This poem depicts the sorrowful dilemmas of two families who have declared war on each other. It includes the Bhagavad Gita mentioned earlier, an important chapter about the god Krishna who, disguised as a charioteer, gives advice to a young warrior named Arjuna, who must go into battle the next day against his own beloved uncles and cousins.

In America, during the Civil War from 1861 until 1865, a number of states tried to withdraw from the United States of America and form another country. Many young American men similar in age to Arjuna had to decide whether to fight in the Civil War when their relatives fought for the opposing side. Families were unhappily divided and many were never reunited. Arjuna's spiritual dilemma about fighting his kinsmen has been reflected for centuries among many people.

The wisdoms found in the Gita, for nearly 2,000 years, provided an avenue of spiritual advice about how to handle the ethical and moral dilemmas concerning the painful demands of war. Even in conflict there were pathways to serve God despite the awful atrocities that occurred during battle. The pathways spoken about in the Gita are specific types of devotional lifestyles. These pathways are called yogas.

Following one or more of the four yogas can help devoted people develop their strengths along their particular path to *moksa*—the liberation from earthly life. Arjuna the young warrior found that his conversations with Krishna, recorded in the Gita, helped him deal with the catastrophic effects of war.

Another popular *smirti* text is the Ramayana. It tells the stories of the hero Rama, a man who is the seventh rebirth of the god Vishnu. Hindus believe that humans, animals, and plants continue to reincarnate after death. Their souls enter a new physical body and they experience the world again. Each new life balances out their past actions, both positive and negative. People live many lifetimes in order to attain spiritual liberation and work out their karma, which is the name for that balance of good and bad. Some gods, too, come back in new cycles of existence as different types of beings, which can include spending lifetimes as various animals.

Many comic books tell about Rama's adventures and the stories

Hindu Music

Hindu devotional songs are called *bhakti* and are being written and sung in all parts of India and America. The poet sages who originally composed these songs to the gods and goddesses were revered. Today the spiritual messages contained in these songs and chants continue to be significant in the rituals of Hindu religious life. Newer songs and chants are added regularly. Web sites and music stores carry CDs of both the modern and classical styles of Indian devotional music.

During the late 1960s and early 1970s the English rock group the Beatles were heavily influenced by Hinduism. Several of the group traveled to India. After Beatles' singer and guitarist George Harrison went to India to study Hinduism and work with a guru, he wrote the popular song "My Sweet Lord." The song can sometimes still be heard on the radio, a legacy from a musician who loved God. Harrison, who died in 2001, found peace and grace in *bhakti*, and it influenced his entire life.

are a favorite of Hindu children. The dramatic epic tells of the importance of marriage vows and loyalty to loved ones.

The Puranas are classified as *smirti* and relate the colorful tales of the gods and goddesses, as well as the legendary ancient heroes. Included in the Puranas are the fascinating creation stories of how the world began and how rebirth occurs. Most religions have some concept of how the world began and in many ways they are similar. Ancient people were intrigued with nature and the development of the planet Earth, the skies, and the seas, as well as with how human life began.

The preservation of *shruti* and *smirti* have helped to sustain the major dimensions of Hindu religious and family life. The stories also pass along Hindu philosophy and mythology. The stories were brought to America through the immigration of revered religious sages, or *rishis*. These men helped found Hindu philosophical schools that have helped Americans take part in an old and revered religious tradition, while giving it a unique twist in a new land.

Hindu immigration to America has added another diverse and interesting dimension to the busy world of religion in America. As the number of followers of Hinduism increased they built temples dedicated to Shiva, Vishnu, and the numerous other gods who are held in high regard. The temples serve as central locations where Hindus can come together to worship during holy festivals and socialize with other Hindus. Temples in America reflect the colorful kaleidoscopic aspects contained in Hinduism while unifying people who are disbursed throughout the American landscape.

Stages of Life and Castes

In classical Hinduism, there were multiple stages of life and various castes. A caste is another name for a special social class that defines one's occupation. The stage of life and caste a person was born into regulated almost every part of his or her life—from clothes to work, to whom a person could marry. In modern Hindu thought, the caste system is beginning to die out or become less of an important factor in determining the course of a person's life, especially in America.

There are four main stages of life in Hinduism. The first is the *brahmacharya* stage. During this stage, the child lives with the family and studies in school. He or she learns skills such as cooking, social manners, and spiritual duties. The stage usually ends in the early 20s.

The second stage is the *grahastha*, or householder stage. In this stage a person will get married, have a family, and build up material wealth for that family. He or she will also make sure that the children are provided for in every way until they have married.

The third stage is the *vanaprastha* stage. This is the retirement stage where the householder leaves the financial duties to his or her children, who are now fully grown. The retiree will stop working and depend on children for support. The retiree will also spend this time in spiritual contemplation and will help care for the grandchildren, especially through spiritual education.

The last stage in a Hindu's life is the *sannyasi* stage. In this stage, the person will retreat completely from the family and will live in nature or go to an ashram (a Hindu place of religious communal living, similar to a Christian convent or monastery) in order to prepare for the next life. Not many modern Hindus end their lives in the *sannyasi* stage, stopping with the *vanaprastha* stage instead. These Hindus become as pious as they can without retreating from their homes and families.

There are also four main castes of Hinduism. The first and highest is the Brahmin caste. This caste is made up almost entirely of priests. The second caste, the *Kshatriya*, is composed of warriors and nobles. The third class is the *Vaishya*, or merchants. The last class is the *Shudra*, or laborers. There are also hundreds of subclasses in Hinduism.

In early times, belonging to a class was part of a person's sacred duty (this duty to the world is sometimes called dharma; see chapter 4 for more information about how belief in dharma affects Hindu believers' everyday lives). In modern times, Hindus are starting to recognize the social injustices that can be incurred with this caste system. Mahatma Gandhi, the great Hindu leader in the struggle to free India from British rule, helped Hindus see the negative aspects of the caste system. Since then, the caste system has been questioned by Hindu populations around the world. It is unlikely that the caste system will be totally abolished in all Hindu groups. However, in America, Hindus are seeking one another out and caste is less of a determining factor for social acceptance than it is in India. Today, professional status is more indicative of whom one associates with or marries. However, some parents in the United States still prefer their children to marry someone from the same caste or region of India.

Hindu Symbols

Hindus have a great number of symbols to represent their faith and practice. These symbols often have many meanings and can be interpreted multiple ways. Here are descriptions of a few of the most important symbols.

The "om" symbol is a sacred mantra (a chant-like Hindu prayer). It is a mantra used in almost every Hindu ritual. It represents life and the very essence of the Ultimate (Brahma).

The swastika has been an ancient Hindu symbol for thousands of years. Unfortunately, German Nazi leader Adolf Hitler used this symbol to represent his Third Reich in the years before and during World War II. The actions of his political regime cost the lives of millions of Jews and other people until the end of that war in 1945. Hitler took the religious symbol from Hinduism and used it for his own political purposes. Because of this, the ancient symbol is associated with horrible actions in modern culture. It was originally a symbol of the sacred in ancient Hinduism, and it is still used for that purpose today by Hindus. Hindus have been appalled at this misuse of their holy symbol for violent atrocities.

Hinduism is a religion full of art. There are many pictures of gods and goddesses; these are called *murtis* (*murti*, in singular form). Each aspect of a *murti* expresses some symbolic meaning of the deity. For example, the creator God Brahma can be shown with multiple heads. This is a symbol of how Brahma can see in all directions.

Everything, including the weapons that the deity carries or is shown within paintings or sculptures; the hand gestures or positions of the hand (*mudras*); and the postures (*asanas*), which can include lying down, sitting, or standing, all have various symbolic meanings. The meaning for each of these things can be complex and relay some important message about the deity. Using pictures and artwork to depict their gods lets Hindus who cannot read know more about their gods and goddesses. They can see the symbolic meaning in the way their deities are depicted in the *murtis* without having to read any stories or even words.

Animals are especially sacred to Hindus. Since the Divine exists in nature, all of nature is Divine, according to Hinduism. This is why there are so many animals in Hindu holy pictures. The cow, in fact, is so sacred in many parts of India that it cannot be harmed and the ani-

mals roam the streets freely. There are even many Hindu gods and goddesses that are part human and part animal, such as Hanuman the monkey god and Ganesha the elephant god.

The Sikhs: Guru Nanak's Special Dream

The early 16th century was a time of political conflict in northern India. The Punjab area in the northeast of India was bitterly fought over by people of different religious traditions, particularly the Hindu and Muslim groups. It was here that Guru Nanak (1469–1539) was born. Distraught about the warfare around him, he dedicated himself to trying to solve the problems between the two groups through thoughts revealed to him while he meditated. Because of his devotion, he experienced a revelation while bathing in a river, and then founded the religion Sikh Dharma.

Guru Nanak's vision portrayed Hindus and Muslims as groups who were not to be separated by faith differences. He believed that his dreams were a bridge between these two diverse, yet neighboring cultures. Knowing that clothing can be an important symbol that

Hair Coverings Are Holy

Today, in the United States, Sikh men may be found in contemporary dress in an attempt to modernize. Some have stopped wearing the traditional cloth or silk turbans they use to wind up their long hair. Some also no longer carry the *kirpan* and the *kach* (see opposite page). Sikh social and religious events encourage the wearing of the turban for the baptized, and turbans are worn in the workplace by those who choose to follow the original precepts of their religion. Even men who cut their hair and no longer wear turbans can still be recognized as Sikhs by the sleek silver bracelet (*kara*) around their wrists.

The turban is not a regular hat. It is a head covering with religious significance. Nearly all of the people in America who wear turbans are Sikhs whose original homeland was South Asia and not the Middle East. Some of the discrimination Sikhs have felt in recent times, most recently following the events of September 11, 2001, has been due to confusion by some people over the meaning of the turbans.

Sikh women in America also may continue to let their hair grow or cut and style it. Colorful scarves may be used for adornment.

Wrapping a Sikh Turban

1. Get a helper to stretch your fabric (which can be 7–8 yards long) with you.

2. Comb your long hair.

3. Twist the hair and tie a knot at your forehead.

4. Hold one end of the fabric between your teeth and tie the cloth once around your head. Follow that pattern. If you slip up the fabric slips off.

5. The last bit of fabric is fastened under the turban in the back of the head.

6. Pull the fabric to cover your head and pull the stump at your neck to tighten the turban.

7. Tidily tuck stray hairs inside the turban.

reveals personal and religious choices, he began to dress in a unique way that blended the traditional garments of both Hindus and Muslims. These garments became an important part of Sikhism. Nanak created a faith that took elements from the people around him.

From Islam he took the name of God, the Ultimate. From Hinduism he borrowed the spiritual ideas about karma, reincarnation (returning to a new life after death), and the steps one takes as a way back to life. Nanak also emphasized the role of the teacher and his teachings as the sole legitimate pathway to the Holy.

After Nanak died, nine other gurus taught after him. The fourth guru, Baba Ram Dass (1534–1581), began construction of the Golden Temple at Amritsar in north India as the most significant holy site for the Sikhs. The fifth guru, Arjan (1563–1606), completed the temple and placed inside it the holy Adi Granth—the collected sacred scripture written by previous gurus. The Golden Temple at Amritsar remains the ancestral home of the Sikh Dharma and is still considered the holiest site for a pilgrimage.

The Five Ks

The 10th guru, Gobind Singh (1666–1708), organized the Sikhs into a special group by forming the Khalsa, the Community of the Pure. Spiritual expression was the focal point of the group. As a sign of unity the men changed their last names to Singh, which means lion, and women took the last name Kaur, meaning princess. Wherever a Sikh goes in the world, they can identify each other by last names.

The five "Ks" are also a unifying factor that enables Sikhs to recognize each other immediately. As a sign of holiness and a pledge to keep their tradition active, the baptized men (*amritdharis*) were to abide by or carry these five Ks:

- *kesh* means allowing the hair and beard to grow long, a sign of saintliness

- *kangh*, a comb especially used for keeping the hair neat

- *kach*, short pants to facilitate quick movement

- *kara*, a steel bracelet to be worn around the wrist signifying restraint

- *kirpan*, a short dagger to be used only in self-defense.

Those Sikhs called *sahajdharis*, or unbaptized, can have short hair and go clean shaven. Also, tobacco and alcohol are not to be consumed by the faithful.

Today, some of the fervent younger members of the Khalsa, in an attempt to distance themselves from their roots, claim that the Sikh tradition has no historical relationship within other religious traditions. However, the union between Hindu and Islamic ideas in the 15th century is evident. Today, emphasis can be placed on Sikh achievements and spiritual focus that have enriched their place in the plurality of religious culture throughout the world and in the United States.

1

East to West: Coming to America

HINDUISM, SIKHISM, AND OTHER LESSER-KNOWN ASIAN RELIGIONS do not have the depth of history that Christianity and Judaism have in America. However, their stories are unique in the world. In no other place in history have so many different religions flourished in one place as they have in America since its earliest days.

Hinduism Comes to America

The history of Hinduism in the United States of America begins long before any gurus (teachers) came to these shores. During the 17th century, missionaries and members of the British government working in India had many sacred texts translated from Sanskrit into English. These books made their way to America. The Bhagavad Gita became a favorite text of the noted American writers Ralph Waldo Emerson (1803–1882) and Margaret Fuller (1810–1850). Along with other leaders of what was called the Transcendentalist movement, they met in New England in the early 1830s and 1840s.

The movement sought to embrace other ideas of the divine beyond traditional Christian models. They looked deeply into Asian thought, including Hinduism and Buddhism. the Hindu idea that "God is One and God is in Everything" appealed to their curious minds. The Transcendentalists' thought of

Hindu Titles

Titles are given to important spiritual teachers by their guru or are bestowed by their followers as a sign of honor. Variations of the name for God may also be found in family surnames or given first names. Some of them are:

Avatar: Incarnation of a great god or spiritual being, especially of the great God Vishnu as Krishna or Rama.

Baba: Means someone who is holy and sometimes is referred to as *Babiji*; ji is a term of honor, endearment, or devotion. For instance, many people called, Gandhi "Gandiji."

Chela: Student of the guru.

Guru: Teacher or spiritual guide.

Mahatma: A title given to a person of great wisdom.

Ram: Name taken from the god Rama; similar to those who name their children Jesus in Spanish.

Rishi: One who has perceived Ultimate Reality or God.

Sadhu: One who has experienced God through meditation.

Swami: Teacher of religious principles.

Yogi: One who practices the yogic methods to reach *moksa* (release from the world).

---

nature itself as holy, a concept not accepted by mainline religions who saw their God as different from and separated from humans. Transcendentalists were against slavery and were early pioneers of social action, in part inspired by ideas from India and other places in Asia.

Another early way that Hindu ideas had an impact in America came through the efforts of an Indian guru named Ram Mohan Roy (1772–1833). He started a group called Bramjo Samaj to transmit to Americans his thoughts about the Upanishads. Roy taught that the highest form of spirituality should be understood without the many colorful deities in other Hindu writings. Roy's first book, *The Precepts of Jesus*, was brought to the United States in 1825. The ideas in the book found some acceptance with the early Unitarians in America. Unitarians thought that God should be worshiped alone and not as a trinity divided into the Father, Son, and Holy Spirit, as many Christian denominations did. The Unitarians and the Bramo Samaj developed close bonds that they continue to share today.

The first Hindu group to travel to America were the members of the Bramo Samaj. Protap Chunder Mazoomdar (d. 1905) of that group gave his first American address on September 2, 1883, at the home of the widowed Mrs. Ralph Waldo Emerson. She had welcomed the trailblazing visit to Concord, Massachusetts. Mazoomdar taught that the highest order of Hinduism was monotheistic. He thought the many gods and goddesses worshiped in Hinduism were of the folk culture and not as important. His teachings about a single God helped attract Americans to this viewpoint because they were familiar with this way of thinking about God.

In 1893, Mazoomdar crossed the seas again to attend the World Parliament of Religions held in Chicago, an international meeting aimed at creating religious friendship. Another prominent Hindu also traveled to speak at this parliament. Swami Vivekananda (1863–1902), a flamboyant speaker and elegant dresser, extolled the benefits of following the teachings of Sri Ramakrishna, an important Indian guru. Vivekananda later founded the Vedanta Society, the first Hindu movement in America. Two of his disciples—Swamis Abhedananda and Turiyananda—came to New York and San Francisco, respectively, to lead the organizations in those two cities. A sprinkling of other

An influential traveler
Jiddu Krishnamurti is shown here on his way via ship to America from India in the 1920s. First touted as a special person by the Theosophical Society, he soon branched out on his own and founded an important school of Hinduism in America.

religious teachers followed these early visitors to the United States. Swami Rama Tirtha, a young monk, arrived in 1902 and lectured in various cities for two years. That same year Baba Prenand Bharati arrived and later organized a group called Krishna Samaj. He left behind followers who were loyal to his teachings well into the 1980s.

Krishnamurti's Influence

An important early group that sponsored Hindu ideas in America was the Theosophical Society, formed in New York City in 1875. The Society rapidly developed groups all over the world, including India. Annie Besant (1847–1933), who became the Society's leader in 1907, spent a great deal of time at one of their sites near Adyar, India. While there, in 1909, she came to believe that Jiddu Krishnamurti (1895–1986), a young Indian boy, was a universal savior who would speak to the world. The Society promoted Krishnamurti as the next *avatar*, or high spiritual being, whose presence would signal the beginning of a new world order. He would teach based on spiritual principles that the Theosophists said were revealed to them by spiritual beings called the Mahatmas, or Great Souls of the invisible world.

Krishnamurti lectured throughout the United States and other countries during the 1920s on behalf of the Theosophist cause and eventually he took up residence in Ojai, California. In the opinions of the Theosophists, he was a figure of enormous significance. Then an unexpected thing happened. In 1927, Krishnamurti renounced his role as a messiah. He became an independent teacher and started a new career apart from the role that Theosophical leaders had chosen for him as a child. He became a forceful guru in his own right, and attracted Americans and people in other countries to hear his message.

In 1925, while aboard a ship bound for Europe, Krishnamurti met a young author named Joseph Campbell (1904–1987). Campbell later became a popular and respected scholar of religion and mythology. His bestselling book, *Hero With a Thousand Faces*, shows how many world cultures share mythologies and religious principles. Campbell's extensive knowledge of Hinduism and his ability to read and translate Sanskrit texts opened new doors for Asian religions in America.

Conversations aboard ship between Campbell and Krishnamurti no doubt strengthened the pathfinding roles each would play here in the United States and in spiritual and educational arenas around the

world. Krishnamurti's popularity inspired people to look for other gurus with spiritual messages to share. Krishnamurti's presence in America fueled the search for individual enlightenment, a search for spiritual education.

Christian Science and New Thought

During the last 50 years of the 19th century, many new religious movements in America were being created. Some included philosophies closer to Hinduism than to religions formed in Europe. The religious freedom available in America helped people decide to seek alternative faiths.

One such group, the Christian Science Association, was formed in Boston in 1875 by Mary Baker Eddy (1821–1910). The Boston area was also the home of the Transcendentalists, who revered the earlier Hindu writings of Mahinder Mohan Roy and later, in 1883, would host Mazoomdar. Christian Science bases much of its ideas about God on

Kumar's Story

Kumar J. is a student of religious studies in Florida; he once trained to be a doctor and is a certified paramedic. He was born in New Jersey of Indian parents and raised in a traditional Hindu household. He tells parts of his story throughout this book to show how one Hindu American has dealt with the challenges and joys of being a part of America.

In elementary school, I noticed how students began forming little groups. I wasn't sure what group to join, and the students often called me names and made fun of me. They made fun of my skin color and the religious articles I wore. My mother and father explained to me at the time that there were not very many Hindus or Sikhs in America, and that sometimes people make fun of that which they don't understand.

My parents taught me a lot about Hindu stories and myths and involved me in religious rituals. They encouraged me to be my Hindu self, even in the midst of others who were different than me. This helped me to appreciate the differences in other students. My grandmother, who lived with us, taught me bhajans (Hindu religious songs) and about gods and goddesses. She often picked me up at school and the kids made fun of her sari (a traditional linen wrap worn by Indian women). She left me with a strong sense of what it was to be a Hindu.

As I got older, I lost my sense of culture and religion for awhile. My family and my Hindu friends helped me reaffirm my identity. In high school, I used my heritage in my studies. Other students began to be receptive to learn about my background. I made a lot of friends who were not Hindu. I was not a strong participant in Hinduism in high school, but I did make an effort to learn more about it and about Indian culture.

As you look at the history of Hindu and Sikh traditions in America, understand how vital and alive our religions are to us.

the *Advaita Vedanta*, a prominent Hindu philosophy advocating the oneness of God. Christian Science also uses the Bible as a main text, along with *Key to the Scriptures* written by Eddy. Some of these religious ideas can be found in parts of the Upanishads.

In 1886 Emma Curtis Hopkins (1849–1925), who had been editor of the *Christian Science Journal* newspaper, left Christian Science and established a new Theological Seminary in Chicago. As the founder of the New Thought movement, she began to teach her version of the religious ideas portrayed in the Advaita Vedanta and contrast them with the Bible. She also used holy texts from many world religions in her writings. Hopkins had extraordinary success and her ideas spread through books, pamphlets, and her nationally-syndicated newspaper column. Later, her students took these teachings abroad.

Inspired partly by Hindu ideas, Eddy, Hopkins, and the Transcendentalists all taught that God is ONE and God is ALL. Because of this, early teachers and gurus from India found some of the groundwork laid for them in parts of America. When a guru named Yogananda arrived in 1922, he mixed ideas from these American-born religions with Hindu philosophy and the idea of positive thinking.

As we will see in chapter 2, a series of events that were more political than religious were the next important steps in the growth of Hinduism in America.

Sikhs in America

As early as 1790 some unnamed Indian visitors, possibly Sikhs, are reported to have landed in Salem, Massachusetts. We will never know what they thought of early America for when they sailed away, it was a long time before explorers from South Asia came to the United States again. In 1897, some Sikhs from the Punjab developed a curiosity about the countries beyond the Atlantic and Pacific oceans, thanks to a trip to England.

Welcome to the West
This photograph from 1905 shows the port of Vancouver, British Columbia, where many Sikhs arrived in the late 19th and early 20th centuries to make a new life in North America.

A Sikh group of musicians from the British Army in India was summoned to England to entertain at the jubilee (50th anniversary) of Queen Victoria. Intrigued by this new culture, the Sikhs decided to tour even farther and explored Canada. They liked the Canadian prairies for farming, work that was a family tradition. These Sikhs went home to India to spread the word about the newly discovered countries.

A group of Sikhs reached Canada in 1903 and by the next year, more than 200 were settled in British Columbia, north of Washington state. Later, some moved to Washington, Oregon, and California. By 1917 there were approximately 7,000 Indians in America and most of them were Jat (agriculturally oriented) Sikhs. They had come to farm and work and send money home to their families in the Punjab in India.

A colorful celebration
Jains are another religious group from India that has formed small communities in the United States. Here, members of the Los Angeles Jain community take part in a celebratory parade.

A Place of Their Own

The first Sikh organization and the oldest gurdwara, which is the Sikh house of worship, in the United States was built in 1912 in Stockton, California. A gurdwara had been built earlier in Vancouver, British Columbia. A Sikh married couple, Jawala and Wisakha Singh, began to have devotional hymns (*kirtan*) sung at their ranch on the Holtville River near Sacramento. Later a building was constructed there that would eventually house the sacred scripture of the Sikhs—the Sri Guru Granth Sahib—and become a temple in 1916. The Pacific Khalsa Diwan Society, founded in 1912 by Sikhs in northern California, became the headquarters for Asian Indians, especially Sikhs, and since 1929 has been an important national Sikh organization in America.

During that time the lumber industry was flourishing and became a unique trade for Sikhs. Owners of the lumber mills hired industrious Sikh men because they had earned a reputation as reliable workers. Their skills and talents as honest workmen helped employers overlook the Sikh's unusual head attire—their turbans. Many Sikhs also worked on the construction of the Western Pacific railroad in California and Utah, a project that was completed in 1909. After that, a number of Sikhs became full-time farmers.

After World War II, another temple was constructed in El Centro, California. More and more Sikhs continued to come to America, and in 1968, the largest Sikh temple in the world was built in Yuba City, California. By the 1980s, more than 250,000 Sikhs lived in America.

The leader of American converts to Sikhism has the title of Yogi Bhajan. This leader is appointed by the Sikh headquarters in Amritsar, India. He teaches his students to rise before sunrise, bathe, and meditate on God's name. Sikhs may be baptized and also become vegetarian. Some of them have opened grocery stores and vegetarian restaurants, popular with health-conscious Americans. Alcohol, tobacco, and illegal drugs are forbidden by Sikhs. They believe these things are bad for the body and take the mind away from its true focus on God.

The Jains Come to America

The Jains are a minority religion which stresses *ahimsa*, non-violent living. There are about about 3 million Jains worldwide, with the greatest number in India. Mahavira (540–468 B.C.E.), the Great Hero, was the original teacher of the ancient Jain religion and he remains a hero

The Zoroastrians

At one time, the Zoroastrian faith spanned vast empires in the ancient world. Today, there are approximately 100,000 Zoroastrians in the world. The founder of Zoroastrianism was the prophet Zarathushtra (known in Greek as Zoroaster), who lived somewhere between 1400 and 1200 B.C.E. in what is today Iran.

Zoroastrians believe in one God, Ahura Mazda. This one God was uncreated, but also has an uncreated opponent, Angra Mainyu. This is an evil Spirit who is just as powerful as Ahura Mazda. The good Spirit, however, created six other Spirits to assist Him in creating the world, and to fight against the evil Spirit. These six good Spirits created the sky, the water, the earth, cattle, plants, good men and women, and fire.

During their stay in Iran, the Zoroastrians (also known as Parsis) were persecuted and had to flee to India. They had a group of 21 holy books, the Avesta. These books were destroyed by Mongolian, Turkish, and Arabian invaders. The only remaining religious texts were commentaries and translations of the texts. Today, the greatest global concentration of Zoroastrians exist on the western coast of India (near Bombay and Sanjan).

The Zoroastrians believe in heaven and hell, the battle between good and evil (with good predestined to win), a resurrection of the dead, the coming of a spiritual Savior, a last judgment by God, and in the verbal inspiration of their holy scriptures. These ideas greatly resemble Christianity and Islam (two major monotheistic religions of the world). Some scholars even believe that Zoroastrianism may have helped develop the religious ideas of these great world monotheisms.

The main center of Zoroastrian worship is in the Fire Temple. It houses the sacred fire, the most pure representation of God. Zoroastrians pray five times each day toward a center of light. In America, a fire is not always accessible, so any source of natural light (moon, sun, lamp flame) is acceptable.

In America and other Western nations, Zoroastrians are facing a challenge. Marrying outside of the religion is strictly forbidden. But finding fellow members of the faith to marry can be difficult. The vast size of America makes this doubly hard for the faithful in this country. Several Internet bulletin boards and Web sites are making use of new technology to make it easier for Zoroastrians to find each other.

Despite the pressures of modern society and the threat of intermarriage, the American Zoroastrian community is surviving, and even accepting many new converts to their faith.

today. There are monasteries in India where Jain monks and nuns who follow the path of *ahimsa* much as the Mahavira originally taught it. There are monks who are skyclad (naked) and remain inside the grounds of the monastery. They believe that clothing harbors tiny insects that may be harmed when they walk or sit down. There are those who are clad in monk's robes who can sometimes go out into the community, but they too are very careful to avoid contact that may kill or injure any living being.

Jains in America are increasing in number every year. There are more than 90 Jain centers and temples in North America. Estimates of the number of Jains are anywhere from 25,000 to 75,000. The first Jain to come to America was Virchand Raghavji Gandhi (1864–1901). He traveled to Chicago in 1893 to attend the first Parliament of World Religions.

Jains are taught to do many things to avoid harming any living being. For instance, they are taught to be strict vegans. They abstain from all animal products, do not hunt or fish, and prefer not to eat fruit or vegetables that are torn from the mother plant. Ideally, they wait for fruit bearing trees to drop their fruit naturally before they use it for a food source.

Some very observant Jains, usually monks or nuns, use brooms to move tiny creatures off walkways to keep from harming them and use strainers to filter drinks so they do not kill any living creatures who may be living in the liquids. Some Jains even wear cloth over their nose and mouth to prevent them from breathing airborne microscopic creatures.

Reverence for all of the inhabitants of the earth is an ethical and moral principle that Jains abide by. Many of those who have immigrated to the United States continue to practice the religion much in the way their ancestors did. They often choose careers as bankers and businessmen in order to remain as far away as possible from the destruction of plant or animal life. A group called Young Jains of America is growing in numbers, and some Jain groups are using the Internet to stay connected to one another. One of the largest groups of Jains is in the Chicago area.

2

Key Events in Hindu and Sikh America

MANY OF THE MOST IMPORTANT EVENTS AFFECTING HINDUS IN America have happened in Washington, D.C. That is, various bills passed by Congress have had an impact on how many Indians could come to this country. At the same time, important events in India have also over time impacted on the Hindu and Sikh communities in America.

Asian Exclusion Act

The growth of Hinduism in America slowed toward the end of World War I due to the Asian Exclusion Act of 1917. This law kept Asians, including Hindus, from coming to America to live. Some Americans and members of Congress, mostly of European origin, thought Asians should be excluded from citizenship because they came from different ethnic and religious backgrounds. Some Asians who were already here feared they would be deported because of their religion and ethnicity.

At the same time, anti-Indian and anti-immigrant riots occurred in the 1920s that were economically motivated. As Asian immigrants were trying to find good jobs and make a living for themselves some Americans feared that they would take the jobs that unskilled American workers might do. It would be a long time before the American justice system recognized the civil rights of the new immigrants. Further, a very negative book by Katherine Mayo called *Mother India*, published in 1927, helped prevent many Americans from developing good relationships with people from India for many years.

Several noteworthy Hindu teachers were able to get in to the United States in this period. For example, Pundit Archarya founded the Temple of Yoga, the Yoga Research Institute, and Prana Press in New York. The most successful of the gurus of this time was Paramahansa Yogananda (1893–1952), who arrived in 1922 to attend a conference. He remained in America afterward and founded the Yogoda-Satsang, known today as the Self-Realization Fellowship, based in Los Angeles. His book, *Autobiography of a Yogi*, was written in 1946 and became a classic still read today. This little book helped spread Hindu ideas into the American religious mix because it incorporated elements of the teachings of Jesus that were compatible with Hindu principles. Yogananda formed a blend of these two traditions that some Americans still cherish.

Hindu Americans had to deal with the Alien Land Law of 1913, which was later added to in 1920-21. This law prevented non-citizens from owning or leasing land on which to farm. Americans who believed the newcomers had been wronged because of their color and religion supported them by leasing the land for the Indian immigrants. As a result of these two pieces of legislation, the Hindu American population plummeted. The 1940 census show that in 1914 there had been 10,000 immigrants from India in California. By 1940 there were just 1,476.

Barriers Ease Slowly

During the late 1930s, the India Welfare League and the Indian League of America lobbied for an end to the ban on Indian immigration and citizenship for Indian peoples. The Atlantic Charter of 1941, a document signed by the United States and Great Britain as a plan for alliance in the coming war, proved to be beneficial in India because the document spoke of the right to self-government. At that time India was still a colony of Great Britain, ruled from London. The United States was afraid that the millions of people in India would support the side of the Axis powers (Germany, Italy, and Japan) during World War II as a way to help expel the British. The American government urged men in India and some women, particularly Sikh women, to serve with the British Military forces, which they did with distinction.

Racial Barriers

In 1922 the Supreme Court made a decision that "white" meant the person was Caucasian and of European ancestry. The designation "white" granted that class of citizens greater rights and privileges in some areas of society. At that time, being "white" allowed a person access to all areas of culture and business; being non-white was sometimes cause for exclusion. This decision lumped immigrants from India and other Asian countries in with African-Americans, already traditionally discriminated against. According to this definition, Hindus were not entitled to the "white" classification because their roots were on the Asian subcontinent and not Europe. After this ruling about 45 naturalized citizens with roots in India were stripped of their citizenship despite the fact that they were responsible residents, settled, and employed.

An important Supreme Court case in 1923 cemented this as a major problem for Indian immigrants. Justice George Sutherland ruled that a man named Bhagat Singh Thind would not be allowed citizenship because of his ethnicity. Sutherland, who was himself an immigrant from England, based his ruling on the Asian Exclusion Act of 1917. Wearing his turban with his uniform, Thind had served in the United States armed forces during World War I but had not served for three years. Anyone serving three years automatically qualified for citizenship in any case, but Thind fell short of this standard.

While continuing to press for his citizenship, Thind attended the University of California at Berkeley until he received his Ph.D. However, the Supreme Court ruling caused major problems not only for him but for other immigrants as well. The *Fresno Morning Republican* and *San Francisco Chronicle* newspapers in California wrote editorials that called Asians low-class and ignorant. The *Chronicle* demanded that Asians who held leases on land be examined by the attorney general of California. Marriage licenses were not issued to some Asian-American couples. The turbulent times continued for Asians until the repeal of the Asian Exclusion Act in 1965. Thind later applied for citizenship in New York and it was granted in 1927.

A government that asked for men and women to serve the American cause by serving in the British military could no longer then exclude such men from U.S. citizenship. Lobbying for Hindu immigration was the successful Sikh merchant Sirdar Jagit "J.J." Singh, who had arrived in America in 1926. He was instrumental in changing some of the immigration laws in a Congressional bill signed in 1946. The new bill provided for a small quota of Indian immigrants per year. It allowed spouses and children of people in the United States to enter the country without counting them against the quota. Between 1948 and 1965, about 7,000 Hindus were allowed to immigrate to America from India.

The Doorway Opens

In 1965, the doorway finally opened all the way. The Asian Exclusion Act was repealed by Congress because it did not allow populations from Asian countries to immigrate to the United States in the same numbers as Europeans. One of the main reasons for the repeal was that America had a shortage of workers in the medical and engineering fields. People with expertise in those fields got first preference for immigration, and this helped create many new Hindu Americans.

A wide variety of Hindu people came from India and other Asian countries after 1965. They enriched the American culture with ideas such as yoga, karma, and dharma. Since then, the many faces of Asian and Hindu philosophy have been able to adapt to a changing America, taking part as equal partners.

The Swinging '60s and '70s

The period following the 1965 repeal of the Asian Exclusion Act was one of rapid growth not only for the number of Hindus who immigrated to America, but also for Hinduism among Americans. The 1960s were a time of experimentation and change in America. Many young people were looking for other ways to live, ways different from those of their parents. The Hindu emphasis on love, community, and freedom appealed to the "flower children" of the era. People also wanted to get more in tune with their inner selves and some of the Hindu meditation practices, such as Transcendental Meditation (known as T.M., see page 90 for more on this discipline), became popular. Several gurus, such as Ram Dass and the Maharishi Mahesh Yogi (see chapter 6 for more on these two teachers), attracted thousands of followers.

INDIA, M.D.

The American Association of Physicians from India was formed in 1982. In 1993, Hindu doctors made up 4 percent of the physicians practicing in America. Their growing influence was shown in 1995, when their annual convention was addressed by President Bill Clinton.

The 1970s were times of further acceptance of Hindu religions and culture. George Harrison of the Beatles was a major player in the transmission of Hindu spirituality to young Americans. Indian sitarist (a sitar is an Indian guitar-like instrument) Ravi Shankar, through his alliance with Harrison, became popular in America and soon around the world. The Hare Krishnas (see the box below) became the most visible of the Hindu groups. Dressed in flowing shawls, they often appeared at airports chanting "Hare Krishna."

The ongoing war in Vietnam was a big issue among America's youth at the time, with many believing that the war was wrong. The Hindu doctrine of *ahimsa*, or nonviolence, became a part of the American anti-war sentiment. Many people made pilgrimages to various Indian shrines to deepen their knowledge of Hindu beliefs and culture, while thousands more joined new Hindu religious movements. If there was a heyday for Hinduism in America, this was the time.

Hare Krishnas

For many Americans, the most visible Hindus are still the orange-robed, often bald Hare Krishnas, sometimes seen on city streets walking and chanting. They are members of the International Society for Krishna Consciousness (ISKCON), based in San Diego. They follow the example of Chaitanya Mahaprabrabhu (1486–1534), who said a path to God can be found through chanting the Hare Krishna mantra (see box).

ISKCON developed in America through the missionary activity of Swami Prabhupada (1896–1977). Prabhupada was a businessman by profession who became an initiate into the Krishna Consciousness movement in India. His guru revealed to him in 1936 that he had an mission to go west to teach Krishna Consciousness. In 1965, he traveled to America and founded a group to spread Krishna Consciousness.

The organization grew and drew attention from the media, who delighted in the colorful appearance of the disciples in their saffron robes dancing around public places, particularly airports, chanting as they danced. The organization received the attention of the anti-cult movement, who tried to keep people from joining such groups. Fear that people would convert to new movements such as this one fueled discrimination toward Krishnas and others. The organization grew in spite of this, establishing centers and finding new followers. Along with their devotions, they became involved in community work, serving the

THE HARE KRISHNA MANTRA

Devotees of the Hare Krishna group chant the following repeatedly as part of their spiritual life. The word "Hare" means "praise," while Krishna and Rama are names of Hindu gods.

Hare Krishna, Hare Krishna

Krishna Krishna, Hare Hare

Hare Rama, Hare Rama

Rama Rama, Hare Hare.

Chanting and praying

Members of the Hare Krishna movement became familiar sights on city streets in the United States starting in the late 1960s. Clad in orange robes and often with clean-shaven heads, they chanted, danced, and played music while raising funds and interest in their community.

poor. ISKCON also gained fame for its colorful festivals. Summer parades were held near ISKCON centers. Bountiful feasts were served to the public.

During the 1980s challenges began to crop up among the Hare Krishna group in a number of ways. Some members of the group argued with other members about their level of devotion to the guru, as opposed to devotion to the principles of the faith. Some devotees spun off, creating smaller organizations. A large group in West Virginia split off as a competing group, with Kirtananada Swami Bhaktipada among its leaders. He constructed a palace in honor of Prabhupada, the original founder, and it became a popular tourist attraction in West Virginia for a time.

Other problems soon arose over the sexual behavior of some members and the use of illegal drugs. There has been controversy over drug dealing and possible stockpiling of guns. In 1987, Kirtananda was indicted for arson, but was acquitted of all charges.

In recent years, another scandal has come up. A $400 million lawsuit charges that ISKCON abused hundreds of children in their boarding schools in the 1970s and 1980s. In 2002, several Hare Krishna temples were facing bankruptcy if they were found guilty.

At its peak of popularity in the 1970s, there were more than 3,000 members who lived communally and about 250,000 lay people involved in devotional worship. Teaching centers and temples can be found in 60 countries around the world. Today, more disciples live at home and travel to festivals or temples. The Hare Krishnas once held a dominant place in American Hindu life, but they have become a shell of their former selves.

Dealing With Discrimination

As first described in the 1923 Supreme Court decision (*United States* vs. *Bhagat Singh Thind*), a person's ethnicity can be an important issue in U.S. legislation and society. As recently as 1980, when several immigrant groups were surveyed in New York City, people from India described themselves as Oriental, Indian, Dravidian, or Caucasian.

Indians in the earlier part of the century appealed to the government to be classified as "white," which they thought would help them with status and prestige. That turned out not to be the best road to follow. When they found out that civil rights legislation would support more equal opportunities for them as minorities, it became advantageous not to be classified white or Caucasian. After Indian groups lobbied for a different classification, the Census Bureau designated Indians, most of whom were Hindus, as Asian Indians. This entitled them to certain protections and benefits that would help them climb the ladder to success.

In spite of some of these benefits, the Hindus in America continued to live with conflict. The Association of Indians in America (AIA) declared to the U.S. Civil Rights Commission in 1975 that they were targets of prejudices. In fact, reports of violence against Indian-Americans cropped up again in the 1980s, as it had done in the 1920s. Those early riots were caused by economic issues; that is, some Americans feared the "foreigners" would come in and take jobs. The more recent crimes seem more racially than economically motivated. In New Jersey, a group of white youths who came to be known as "dot busters" (so named for the *bindhis*, or painted dots, worn on the forehead of some Hindus; see chapter 3) killed a number of successful Hindu men. Hate crimes such as these happen when the person is angry inside and acts out the anger against innocent people. Hindus and other minorities continued working to find a place in America—a place where they could be safe and secure while honoring their ethnicity and religion.

Gandhi's Impact

Perhaps the most famous Hindu person in America was not an American at all. Mahatma Mohandas Gandhi (1869–1948) was the leader of the peaceful revolution that helped India earn its freedom from Britain in 1948. Mahatma is an honorary title, which means in Sanskrit "great soul." Gandhi was a teacher of *ahimsa* (nonviolence) and is remembered still by those who use peaceful negotiation to deal with conflict.

He is remembered in a number of ways in the United States. An elementary school in Jersey City, New Jersey, is named for Gandhi. Statues of Gandhi can be found in a number of American cities including Atlanta and New York. The U.S. government has approved construction of a memorial to Gandhi to be built in the diplomatic area of Washington, D.C., not far from the memorials to Abraham Lincoln and George Washington. The costs will be borne by the Indian Government and various Hindu groups in America.

Gandhi's work for the equality of all religions and ethnic groups, while not conducted specifically in America, has served as a model for methods of peaceful non-violence in all countries. His moral stance and ethical actions showed India it could be free from foreign rule without using force and increasing the bloodshed and human suffering.

In 1998, a major Indian group in the United States marked the 50th anniversary of the assassination of Mahatma Gandhi and the 30th anniversary of the assassination of the Reverend Martin Luther King, Jr., whose civil rights leadership in the 1960s was in part inspired by Gandhi's example of nonviolent resistance. This event was the first to recognize the similar, difficult experiences that both African-American and Hindu Americans endured when their heroes were killed.

Bhagwan Shree Rajneesh

In the 1980s, a group founded by Indian guru Bhagwan Shree Rajneesh was very influential among American Hindus, but a financial scandal

Two for freedom
During his nonviolent campaign against British rule, Mahatma Gandhi, right, worked closely with Jawaharlal Nehru, who would become the first president of the new nation of India in 1948. Gandhi is today recognized as an inspirational figure in the history of nonviolent civil disobedience.

helped remove him from his own organization. Rajneesh, also known as Osho, was a controversial teacher who traveled to the West. As a young man in college in 1953, he experienced *samadhi*, or enlightenment bliss. He eventually earned a masters degree in philosophy and sharpened his skills as a lecturer and teacher by accepting public speaking engagements throughout India. In the early 1970s Rajneesh began to initiate people into his philosophy and practices that significantly departed from Hindu customs. Rajneesh taught that the real path to spiritual enlightenment is to stay in the world, enjoying life to the fullest while not being attached to it.

In the Hindu viewpoint, attachment to the world means that one is captured by pleasures instead of seeking spiritual liberation from

A controversial spiritual leader

Bhagwan Shree Rajneesh was at one time perhaps the most famous Hindu spiritual leader in America. However, immigration problems and financial irregularities forced him from his work and eventually out of the country.

the world. Rajneesh gained converts and alienated traditional schools of Hinduism. He asked his followers to dress in orange, the traditional color of a monk's robes. They also received a new name and were required to meditate for at least an hour a day. Many americans discovered Rajneesh in 1972 when he visited America to talk about philosophy.

Rajneesh immigrated to the United States in 1981 and moved to a huge ranch in Oregon. His "city" there was called Rajneeshpuram, and it became a headquarters and commune for his followers. Sometimes there would be as many as 5,000 people there. The local ranchers thought he was not a good neighbor. Local Christian fundamentalist people and groups, who did not agree with his teachings, also did not like having him around.

At one point Rajneesh had a fleet of 93 Rolls Royces and had invited thousands of street people to live in his commune. He expected them to establish residence and vote in the local elections. The federal government and Oregon state officials began to take a look at Rajneesh's operation as complaints rose about his lifestyle.

In 1985, Rajneesh accused his secretary, Ma Anand Sheela, of crimes against his devotees and called the police. He was astonished when a few weeks later federal agents came to arrest him and charged him with immigration violations. He was deported. The Oregon commune crumbled and became a ghost town.

Rajneesh returned to India, and revived his commune there in 1987 as an international site for his followers. He had attempted a world tour in 1986, but, due in part to U.S. government efforts, he was refused entry into 21 countries. In 1988 he changed his name to become known simply as Osho, a Japanese term of endearment for a spiritual master. Osho became ill and suffered through a puzzling array of symptoms. His followers claimed he was poisoned while in U.S. custody. He died in 1990.

Awards and Honors for Hindu Americans

In 1968, the Nobel Prize was awarded to Har Gobind Khorana of the University of Wisconsin at Madison for important experiments in medicine and physiology. Subramanyam Chandrasekhar of the University of Chicago won a Nobel Prize in 1983 for innovations in physics. Their accomplishments point to the many contributions of Hindu Americans in the sciences.

But science is not the only area in which Hindu Americans have excelled. Amartya Sen won the 1998 Nobel Prize for major contributions to welfare economics. In 1996, he became the first Hindu president of the American Economic Association.

In 2002, for the first time, a Hindu American scholar was elected to lead a major American religious studies group. Vasudha Narayanan is president of the prestigious American Academy of Religion, an international organization with more than 7,000 members from all over the world.

Technology Drives Immigration

Today, the major area of influence among Indian Hindus in America is in technology. The number of Indian immigrants working in the burgeoning high-tech industry in the 1990s was greater than almost any other minority group except for other Asian immigrants. Not only were they involved as skilled workers, but they also began to become entrepreneurs, helping to start companies and rising to important executive positions. It was a long way in only a century from being declared illegal immigrants to being welcomed as major contributors to America's economy.

They also became significant contributors to India's economy. Many Indian immigrants who settled in California's Silicon Valley, home of many high-tech and Internet companies, reached back to India to help, using their new-found wealth. A growing number of Indian-Americans helped to fund similar start-up companies back in India, while others were meeting with Indian government officials to find out how they could help. Some people think that so many highly educated people leaving a country can be a problem for the economy of that country, but this reaching out by Indian Americans proves that success can be a two-way street.

Sikhs Affected by September 11

Perhaps no other time in the history of the United States have the Hindu and Sikh communities been struck so deeply as after the terrorist attacks on the United States on September 11, 2001. It quickly became apparent that the terrorists had roots in Arab nations. Unfortunately, Americans who were angry and confused acted out against innocent Sikh, Hindu, and Arab people who were not responsible for the events of that day.

There were deadly attacks by Americans upon some people of color. In Arizona, a Sikh man was shot one morning when he opened up his gas station. He wore a turban in the Sikh style, but his attackers believed him to be Arab. Of course, it is not right to attack anyone no matter what they wear, but the added tragedy here was that attackers had misidentified their perceived enemy. Sikh men are recognized by their turbans and beards which are required by their religion. Tragically, some Americans think they are associated with the Taliban, who

Speaking for Sikhs
*As part of an interfaith serv-
ice following the tragedy of
September 11, 2002,
Trilochan Singh spoke at a
Presbyterian church in Florida. In the aftermath of the
attacks, some Sikhs had
been attacked by people
mistaking them for Arabs.*

wear headgear that looks like a turban. It is cold in Afghanistan and
headgear is worn to repel the cold and is not tied in the same way the
Sikh religious turban is. Sikhs are also not from the same regions of
the world as the Taliban.

As a result of that murder and similar actions, the Sikhs have
formed groups such as the Sikh American Association and the Sikh
Coalition (see page 95) to help. In October 2001, Senator Richard Dur-
ban (D-Illinois) introduced a bill that condemned bigotry and violence
against Sikh Americans. The bill says that local law enforcement au-

thorities must prosecute to the fullest extent of the law all those who commit crimes against Sikh Americans. Sikh leaders such as Amrith Kaur and Gurpreet Singh, senior delegates of the Sikh American Association, supported the bill.

One Hindu's Thoughts

Kumar J. (see page 30) relates his experiences after the terrorist attacks of September 11.

After September 11, I heard about attacks on Hindu and Sikh people by Americans angered about the actions of the terrorists. I didn't really believe those stories until they began happening to me.

I began to notice a lot of people acting differently. I noticed how people talked about me and pointed because I was carrying a book on Hinduism, or because I was walking with some of my Muslim friends, who wore religious head coverings. One time, I asked these people why they sneered at me.

"We do not like terrorists!" they said. I was dismayed. These people had equated me, a person of Indian descent, with a network of terrorists. Is it because I looked different than them? They did not even know me, yet they assumed things about me that were not true.

In the following months, I volunteered to walk my female Muslim friends to their cars after dark. It is a horrible feeling to know that people may be out to harm you. Most people who are prejudiced against someone else do not really know much about that other person. Yet once you get to know that person, you may find that they are not much different from yourself.

Events of the Year

Various festivals honoring Hindu gods and goddesses dot the annual calendar of Hindus, both in America and elsewhere. In India, the calendar is based on a lunar year of 11 months, but Hindus in America use the standard 12-month solar calendar as well. These festivals vary among different types of Hinduism, and there are some that are celebrated in India but not in the United States. Also, Hindus do not celebrate a Sabbath as Christians and Jews do, for instance; however, Mondays are special days for the worship of Shiva.

From among the many festivals and holidays, here are examples of major events:

Vasant-Panchmi (January or February) is a special day for students. The holiday is held to honor Saraswati, the goddess of learning and knowledge. Some Hindu students in America even create their own prayer day to Saraswati before taking important tests.

Shivaratri (February or March) is a celebration of Shiva, one of the Hindu Trimurti (three main gods). The major Shiva festival in India and America, it is celebrated with songs, *pujas*, and joyous activities.

Raksha Bandhan (July or August) is a holiday for brothers and sisters. A sister will tie a *rakhi* (a special cloth or metal bracelet) on her brother's wrist to honor him. Her brother will then give her a gift and promise to protect her. Sometimes in America if a Hindu boy or girl does not have a sister or brother, they will exchange gifts with a Hindu friend.

Janmasthtami (August or September) celebrates Lord Krishna. Fasting and praying are common for this celebration. This is a very important holiday for the Society for Krishna Consciousness (ISKCON; see pages 41–43) in America.

Diwali (October or November) is the official Hindu and Indian New Year and lasts for five days. Butter and oil lamps are lit in all Hindu American homes. Hindus wear new clothes. This day also celebrates the god Rama's victory over a demon king Ravana (in the epic story called Ramayana). Lakshmi, the Hindu goddess of fortune, will come into a Hindu home at night and bless it if the Hindu home is clean. For Hindus, cleaning their homes is of the utmost importance at this time.

Holi (February or March) is a fun holiday when all caste or social rank is forgotten. People wear old clothes and throw colored powder on each other (photo above). In America, young Hindus use water guns to squirt colored liquids, too.

Sikhs often celebrate similar holidays as Hindus. One special Sikh holiday is Guru Nanak's birthday in November. Sikhs celebrate this holiday, but it is sacred for some Hindus as well. In America, festivities are held in gurdwaras and in Hindu temples.

3

Hindus and Sikhs in American Culture

HINDUS AND SIKHS HAVE HAD MANY DIFFERENT INFLUENCES ON the United States. The Hindu and Sikh traditions have contributed a complex medical system, which incorporates yoga and the chakra system. Hindu and Sikh fashions have become a part of American culture in many ways. Literature in America has also been influenced by Hindu thought and by many Indian writers. Traces of the Hindu and Sikh traditions appear at many different levels of American popular culture, from Madonna concerts to major movies to a character on *The Simpsons*. Finally, the Internet has contributed significantly to the understanding and spread of Hindu and Sikh culture.

Hindu Medical System

Thousands of years ago, Hindus created a medical system known as Ayurveda (pronounced *ah-yur-VAY-da*, it means "life knowledge"). This system is in use to this day in India, and is gaining more and more popularity in America. Before we examine its influence in America, let us have a look at the principles of Ayurvedic medicine.

Ayurveda is actually a Hindu text that comes from the Atharva Veda, one of the four holiest books of Hinduism. Ayurveda is a holistic system of medicine, which means it looks at the total human being, not just one illness or injury. It also addresses psychological illnesses as well as physical ones. Ayurveda is also a preventive medical system. This means it is practiced daily to prevent illness rather than working on ways to cure illness (though it does that as well). Because of this, Ayurveda is a way of living as well as a medical system.

Ayurveda says that there are three *gunas*, or qualities, that comprise the essence of a person. The three *gunas* are *sattva*, *rajas*, and *tamas*. *Sattva* is purity and pleasure and is associated with the mind. *Rajas* is activity and motion. This *guna* is associated with the physical aspects of a person. *Tamas* is in opposition to *rajas*, therefore it means one becomes inactive. A person can have a deficiency in *sattva* and have difficulty concentrating, according to Ayurveda. Each person usually has a combination of each. A balance between the three is essential to achieving complete health. Too much imbalance between any of the *gunas* can lead to physical or psychological illness.

A second major idea of Ayurveda is the three basic forces of nature: *vatta*, *pitta*, and *kapha*. *Vatta* controls physical movement. If *vatta* dominates a person's inner forces, they could be prone to restlessness, according to Ayurveda. *Pitta* controls the ways the body breaks down substances and body temperature. If *pitta* dominates a person's inner forces, they are very intelligent, and are also quick to move around. *Kapha* controls the physical frame of a person and their psychological temperament. If *kapha* dominates a person's inner forces, they are said to be calm, pleasant people who tend to gain weight easily.

According to Ayurveda, there are 10 different combinations of these forces, or ten different types of people. After an Ayurvedic physician diagnoses the type of forces and the *gunas* a patient is comprised of, the physician can then prescribe herbs and other remedies to treat illnesses associated with that combination.

Ayurveda in America

Today in America, there is much public interest in Ayurveda. Major health food stores and even some specialty supermarkets have sections of Ayurvedic herbs and medicines. Medical schools sometimes offer elective courses in alternative medicine, including Ayurvedic medicine. Popular authors such as Dr. Andrew Weil have attested to the benefit of Ayurveda. Another well known proponent of Ayurveda is Dr. Deepak Chopra (see the box on page 55).

PRECEDING PAGE
Ancient dance in America
This young dancer performs an ancient Indian dance, but she is doing it in Seattle, Washington. Indian and Hindu culture have become an important part of the American mosaic.

Vasant Lad has pioneered Ayurvedic medicine in the United States. In 1984, Lad founded The Ayurvedic Institute in Albuquerque, New Mexico to teach Americans about Hindu forms of healing. It also serves as a place to learn Sanskrit. The Institute holds classes, has a correspondence course, teaches public seminars, has a therapeutic clinic, sells books and Ayurvedic practitioner items, and publishes a quarterly journal, *Ayurveda Today*.

The National Institutes of Health (NIH) has a special division for the study of holistic and alternative medical therapies. The NIH, a division of the U.S. Department of Health and Human Services, has spent millions of dollars in the study of Ayurvedic medicine. Projects include Ayurvedic anti-malarial treatments, herbal clinical trials, and research projects with Ayurvedic medicinal researchers in India.

Deepak Chopra

Deepak Chopra, a medical doctor from India, has become very famous in America by teaching a mix of Ayurvedic medicine and Hindu philosophy to Americans. His books present Hindu thought in a manner that can be adapted and practiced in American culture. His works have been used in personal study, and large corporations have also used his ideas in helping employees improve themselves.

His book *How to Know God* (published in 2001) has brought the Hindu concept of religious pluralism to the popular American audience. Pluralism is the idea that all religions have merit and truth to them. He teaches that God can be found in everything, including in nature, people, and animals.

Chopra's books have found a vast audience in America where there is a great diversity of religious beliefs and practices. He also runs a center in California where students learn about the healing practices of Hinduism and other Asian religions.

It is not all this hard
Yoga has become very popular in America with both Hindu Americans and non-Hindus. Using ancient forms of movement and breathing, yoga practitioners move into different poses or forms. Many people, from pregnant women to top professional athletes, have used yoga to improve their overall health.

Eat Your Vegetables

An important aspect of the Hindu medical system is vegetarianism. All schools of Hindu medicine recommend vegetarianism and/or veganism. The former is a diet that does not include meat, poultry, or fish, but only vegetables, fruit, dairy, and grains. Vegans do not eat animal products of any kind, including eggs or dairy products. In Hindu and Sikh thought, eating the flesh of other creatures will not benefit people in their attempt to be physically fit.

In light of the way the meat industry uses growth hormones, preservatives, and antibiotics, some Americans feel this style of eating is a healthy option. The American Vegan Society upholds this opinion of non-violence toward animals. Some of the animal rights activism and the move to vegetarian diets in this country is partially due to the influence of Hindu ideas on American culture beginning in the 1960s.

To supplement their protein intake, vegans and vegetarians eat protein-rich beans and legumes and sometimes take protein supplements. This position of *ahimsa* (nonviolence) towards animals, according to Ayurveda, is also good for the psychological self. Ayurvedic practitioners claim that the mind can function better if it knows that it has not contributed in any way to the killing of animals.

Yoga

Yoga is probably the most obvious Hindu contribution to the American lifestyle. It has spread widely in America today and has become a recognized part of American culture. Almost every major city has yoga centers or yoga workshops. Though originally created as a Hindu spiritual exercise, yoga has become integrated so much into American culture that it has taken other forms. Americans of any religious background value yoga for its exercise benefits without necessarily believing in or practicing the spiritual dimensions of yoga.

Yoga, a Sanskrit term, means "union." The main text for the study of yoga is the Yoga Sutras, a collection of teachings by the great yogi (one who practices yoga) Patanjali, who lived in the second century B.C.E. in India. Yoga uses a variety of techniques and traditions in the Hindu and Sikh traditions. There is no one form of yoga, there are many forms. The goal of all yogas, however, is the same: to bring the person to a state of Oneness with their object. The object can be God, another person, themselves, or anything else they meditate about.

Yoga combines physical poses with special kinds of breathing, usually done by breathing in through the nose and out through the mouth. Students work with teachers who help them concentrate their minds and move through breathing and physical movements properly. Although it can look simple, yoga can be a very strenuous workout.

Most major universities offer yoga classes in their physical education or dance departments. Professional athletes now sometime include yoga in their workout routines to help them improve flexibility. Young people also often do yoga, and many schools now include it in their P.E. classes.

Chakras and the Body

The chakra system is the foundation through which yoga works. Each chakra, or energy center, is considered to govern a set of glands within the human body. Ayurvedic medicine says that humans and all life forms show energy patterns from specific areas of the body. Normally, these centers, or chakras, can not be seen except by those who see auras

YOGA FOR EVERYONE

Yoga can be a strenuous workout for very active students of the discipline. However, yoga postures or movements can be made gentler for young people, the elderly, or those with physical challenges.

In schools and in many yoga classes, too, the religious aspects are not always emphasized. This way everyone can feel free to participate in this health-enhancing activity.

Yoga Can Help Your Grades!

More and more schools are including yoga among their P.E. choices. Kids as young as three or four can enjoy the poses, while older kids say they can increase their level of concentration in class and improve their grades. Annie Buckley teaches yoga to kids in Los Angeles and has created a deck of cards showing poses young yoga fans can try. Here are some of the things she tells her students:

In yoga, there are many different positions that you can do with your body. The idea is to breathe during each of these positions as calmly as if you were sitting on the floor. This helps you to have a stronger and more flexible body, but it is also good for your mind and emotions. Also, some people think that yoga is very quiet and mellow. It is true that yoga is generally a slow and solitary activity. But the purpose of yoga is to achieve balance. That means you include active, fun, loud times as well as quiet and reflective times.

Yoga can help you do better on tests. It teaches you how to calm down and to focus. You learn for yourself how to do this. The best way to understand yoga is to try a little bit yourself. Read this over and then try it out.

First, sit comfortably. Take deep breaths in and out. Feel your lungs expand as you inhale and get smaller as you exhale. Try closing your eyes and feeling the breath come in and out.

Then try covering your ears and listen to the sound of the breath. Take 10 deep breaths and count them out on your fingers. This is a good thing to practice before a test or some other stressful event.

or energy fields that surround the body. Those who see these auras report that they look like rainbows shifting colors. When a person is sick or has been hurt, these energy fields change color and shape. The goal is to regulate these chakras for maximum physical health.

According to Ayurveda, each individual has points of spiritual energy that can be released through special meditations in yoga. Each of these seven chakras in the human body has these specific roles:

• **Muladhara**	base of the spine	body wastes
• **Svadhistana**	below the navel	breath
• **Manipura**	at the navel	sight
• **Anahata**	at spine in front of heart	touch
• **Vissudha**	behind the throat	hearing, creativity
• **Ajna**	between the eyebrows	the mind
• **Sahasraha**	top of the head	the spirit

Susumna is the major "vein" of the body (the spinal cord) by which the spiritual energy (*kundalini*) created through meditation and yoga travels. The *kundalini* energy remains coiled at the base chakra like a serpent. It awaits the signals to become uncoiled. When a person uses special meditations aimed at awakening *kundalini* power, it becomes uncoiled. As the *kundalini* energy becomes aroused and travels upward through the body it engages each chakra from lower to higher giving it permission to activate. The corresponding senses energized by that specific chakra become invigorated and operate at peak efficiency. When the aroused *kundalini* power reaches the top most chakra, the Sahasrara, the individual supposedly acquires profound spiritual, mental, and physical powers and achieves bliss.

Astrology

Astrology is the study of stars, star patterns, planets, and the solar system as a way to predict tendencies toward personal or group behavior or attitudes. The Hindu form of astrology has gained popularity in America. Along with the stars, the planets are very important to this astrological system in both the Hindu and Western systems. Palm reading is also important in Hindu astrology.

There are 12 signs in the Hindu Zodiac, as there are in the Western system. There are also the days of the week. The days regulate the daily lives of people. For instance, Sunday, Tuesday, and Saturday are unlucky days, on which no new business or journey should be started. Hindu business men and women in America sometimes keep this in mind when starting new business deals or when planning business trips.

The stars and planets or signs evident during the day that a person is born will actually represent one of the deities that a Hindu child is supposed to worship. For example, if the Hindu child is born under the sign of the planet Saturn, he or she is supposed to pay homage to the Hindu deities that are associated with that planet. Such actions will assist in a long and happy life, according to some Hindu texts.

Hindu astrology and palmistry have become even more important in America because there are not many Hindu priests in the United States. If Hindus need to know that they are honoring the gods and goddesses in the right way, they can use a professional astrologer to help them figure out what actions to take. There are many ads for Hindu

CHAKRAS AND SPIES
In America, practitioners of yoga often include the chakra system in their study. Some American scientists, as well as the Russians, have also studied the chakra system for its possible therapeutic or diagnostic uses. There are personal accounts that suggest that the U.S. government as well as the former Soviet Union have trained people who see the aura or chakra system to use these skills in espionage assignments. Today, it remains a mystery whether any spies can indeed read the chakra system well enough to use it.

astrologers in popular Indian magazines such as *India Abroad*, an international magazine aimed at Hindu Americans and Sikh Americans.

Sometimes a Hindu family consults an astrologer about the health and destiny of a future child. Before the child is born (usually while a woman is in advanced stages of pregnancy), an astrological chart may be designed for the child. The astrologer may ask the parents about various aspects of their lives to help determine insights into their child's future life. The chart can be completed when the child is born. The child's date, time, and place of birth are used, along with the circumstances surrounding the birth. The chart is supposed to help the parents plan for the marital, career, emotional, educational, spiritual, and physical future of the child. This practice is not as widely practiced in America as it is in India, but it is gaining more attention.

Hindu Skin is "In"

The colorful and flowing clothing of India came to America with the arrival of Hindus from that country. Some of the fashion has influenced what Americans wear. One of the most popular Hindu-inspired fashions has nothing to do with clothing, however.

Henna is a special plant grown in India. This plant can be picked, dried, crushed, and ground into a fine powder. The fine powder is made into a paste mix. When the paste mix is applied to the skin and left to dry, it forms a temporary tattoo that lasts about one to two weeks. Henna is used primarily by women, but men in America have used it as well.

A special design, usually religious, is chosen and drawn on the skin, usually the hands, feet, and face. Henna comes in many shades of red and orange. Henna is also used as a hair dye in some American beauty products. Henna was originally used as sacred adornment for brides and bridesmaids in Hindu weddings. There are Indian beauty shops in America that specialize in these types of cosmetic arts. In Hindu and Sikh culture in America, women sponsor "henna parties." Usually a henna artist will be hired to apply specific designs for the women at the party while they socialize.

Another Hindu fashion statement is *kajul*, a special kind of eye liner. *Kajul* is used in India as an eye liner for girls and boys to ward off the "evil eye." The concept of the evil eye is found in many parts of the world. It is an ancient idea that there are people who can look at children and something bad will happen to them. In India the solution

A MATE IN THE STARS

Because Hindu Americans count the practice of astrology in helping to guide one's life among their traditions, some families use the star charts to help them find the right husband or wife for their children. Ads in Hindu newspapers and magazines might mention the birth sign of the prospective bride or groom, along with information about their age and profession.

Hands up for henna
Beautiful designs made with henna stay on a person's skin for weeks or months. Wearers use traditional Indian designs or create their own patterns. Even non-Hindu American women have added henna to their list of beauty aids.

to the problem of the evil eye is the drawing of *kajul* around the eyes of little ones. It comes in eyeliner and in powder form. Some American women use *kajul* as another kind of unique makeup around their eyes. In the United States, *kajul* is used for beautification only, not as protection from the evil eye.

Bindhis and Beads

A common feature of many Hindu women is the dot on their foreheads. This dot was originally a religious symbol with many meanings. It can represent Shiva, whose third eye is closed, showing self-control. It can also represent Durga, a Hindu goddess, or Vishnu. Men also wear this religious symbol, as do some Jains, Buddhists, and Sikhs. It used to be made by applying a colored powdery paste to the forehead.

Women have turned this religious symbol into a fashion statement. They created little stickers, with beautiful designs and sometimes bits of jewels. This reusable sticker is called a *bindhi*. When immigrants from India came to America, women here adored the *bind-hi* and companies began creating them for the American marketplace. Today, sheets of *bindhis* of various colors are for sale in many beauty stores. Gwen Stefani, lead singer of No Doubt, sometimes wears a *bindhi* when performing.

Indian jewelry has also become very popular in America. Jewelry is a religious symbol for Hindus as well as for Sikhs. Some Sikh men wear a sparkling silver bracelet called the *kara*, one of the "five Ks" (see page 23). Many precious stones (such as diamonds, rubies, and emeralds) are said to have special healing auras and powers. Ayurvedic practitioners tell Hindus which jewels they should and should not wear for their health. Hindus have often believed that jewelry has healing qualities. The more pure the jewelry, the more powerful it is. This is why many Hindu women do not wear costume jewelry. Jewelry selection has become a way for Hindus and Sikhs living in America to identify with their ancestral homeland.

In the 1970s many young people in America were seen wearing beads, usually made of wood and tied into a necklace. They were inspired by Hindu prayer beads, called *malas*. A traditional Hindu *mala* is made of sandalwood or stone and contains 108 beads. Sikhs use *malas* too, though theirs can be made of other substances, and they can have different numbers of beads. A *mala* is used to count prayers, much in the same way that a Roman Catholic would use a rosary to pray and count prayers. In America, *malas* are used for that purpose, but also have a decorative purpose when worn around the neck.

Indian Writers on the Rise

Hinduism has melded into mainstream American literary trends. The Bhagavad Gita is sometimes used as literature in American schools. The ISKCON movement has even used it to spread their teachings, thus furthering awareness of Hindu writings. Such American writers as Ralph Waldo Emerson and the Catholic mystic Thomas Merton (1932–1968) have woven Hindu ideas into their works. Dr. Martin Luther King Jr. used Mahatma Gandhi's speeches about *ahimsa* as one inspiration for his nonviolent resistance to racial injustice.

In recent years, many Indian writers have found success and fame in America, often using their novels to tell about life in India in both past and present times. Arundhati Roy's *The God of Small Thing*s

TINY BELLS

A popular type of Hindu jewelry is an ankle bracelet with little bells (called *payal*). When women in Hindu temples worshiped, they wanted to make sure the gods and goddesses were awake and listening to their prayers. They invented ankle bracelets with little bells to get their attention when they prayed and did devotional dances. The gods and goddesses were also supposed to take notice of the worshiper whenever she entered the temple because her jewelry made a pleasant sound for them. When *payal* came to America with Hindu and Sikh immigrants, American women made it popular here as costume jewelry. The bells are often made in silver, but come in gold versions, too.

was a success with critics and readers. Jhumpa Lahiri, Bharati Mukherjee, Manil Suri, and Amitav Ghosh are among novelists who have received acclaim. C.K. Prahalad and Deepak Chopra have written popular nonfiction titles. As one editor pointed out, with all those millions of people in India who speak English, there were bound to be some fine writers among them.

Entertainment and Popular Culture

Hinduism has made a big impact on American music, especially since the 1960s. One of the first and most important Hindu influences was Ravi Shankar, a world renowned Hindu sitarist and singer. The sitar is a stringed instrument similar to a guitar or a lyre. His work is reflective of classical and folk music found in Hindu culture. The Hindu *bhajan* (devotional song to a God) has been widely used by Shankar in his music. Shankar has brought ancient Hindu chants to modern America and he has had a notable influence on some of the Beatles' music later in their career. Shankar, now in his 80s, has won Grammy awards, played all over America and the world, and produced dozens of CDs. Shankar, while innovative, is still primarily a traditional musician attempting to preserve Hindu music.

Indipop works harder to mix modern music with traditional Hindu forms. Sheila Chandra is a pioneer of Indipop in Great Britain and brought her music to America in the late 1980s. Chandra combines American contemporary music with Hindu chants, Indian style, and sometimes other cultural influences.

The younger generation of Hindus and Sikhs in America has continued this blending of American and Indian music. These artists mix rap, techno, and dance music with the familiar sounds of traditional Indian music. Even *bhajans* have been set to a contemporary rhythm by some of these artists. DJ Romy and others spread this trend among young Hindus and Sikhs in this country. Tony Kanal, the bass player for No Doubt, is one of the relatively few individuals of Indian descent working actively in American pop music.

The Sikh tradition has introduced religious music that has taken root in America. One example of popular Sikh music is the Spirit Voyage Music company, based in Virginia. This company, a key player in international music, promotes the work of Sikh Americans such as Snatam Kaur, Livtar Singh, and Guru Ganesh Singh.

RAVI SHANKAR

More than any other single artist, sitarist and composer Ravi Shankar (b. 1920) is responsible for the impact of Indian music in America. In the 1960s, already one of India's top traditional musicians, he brought his ancient instrument and modern approach to music to America. Shankar performed at Woodstock, at the Monterey Pop Festival, and other concerts not normally associated with Indian music. The Beatles were among the many famous musicians who studied with, were inspired by, and performed with Shankar. Today, Shankar's daughter Anoushka performs with him, continuing the family tradition.

Rock god
No Doubt bassist Tony Kanal (right, performing with lead singer Gwen Stefani) is one of a handful of Indian Americans active in today's rock music scene.

Movies and Television

India produces more movies than any other country in the world. Bollywood, as the Bombay-centered film industry is called, is as popular in India, if not more so, than Hollywood is in the United States So it is not surprising that Hindu and Sikh ideas and themes have found their way into American entertainment. In the movie *Indiana Jones and the Temple of Doom*, for instance, the hero battled the ancient Kali cult. Kali is a Hindu goddess who protects her followers and destroys spiritual forces that try to prevent the understanding of truth.

Other Hindu stories, such as the Ramayana and Mahabharata epics, have been turned into dramatic mini-series in Great Britain and are seen in America as well. In addition, some popular Indian movies such as *Kabhi Khushi Kabhie Gham*, an epic adventure story, have English subtitles so that the American audience can enjoy these contemporary classics as well. Sagar's 27-part video of the Ramayana epic became an immediate Hindu contemporary classic. It too has English subtitles and has contributed greatly to the American understanding of this legendary Hindu epic.

Several Indian-themed or Indian-made movies have had success either at the box office or among movie critics. In 1992, the American-made *Mississippi Masala* by director Mira Nair told the story of a Hindu girl (Sarita Choudhury) falling in love with a non-Hindu American (Denzel Washington), a theme important to Hindu Americans. In recent years, more and more Indian films have made big splashes in America. The producers James Ivory and Ismail Merchant have teamed with screenwriter Ruth Prawer Jhabala to create several award-winning films, including *Passage to India*. In 2002, the film *Monsoon Wedding* played to critical and popular acclaim around the United States.

Hinduism is also becoming more visible on television. The ABC comedy *Dharma and Greg* uses a Hindu concept for a main character's name (no, it is not Greg). In the show, Dharma (played by Jenna Elfman) is a young yoga instructor. She was raised by hippie parents, who contributed to her interest in yoga and other Hindu ideas. Dharma marries a man who is the exact opposite of her, yet they are a perfect match. Americans are obviously interested in the "East meets West" concept, since the show has been running successfully since 1997.

The Simpsons frequently includes segments with Apu, an Indian immigrant who settled in America and opened up a quick-stop market. Though the show often depicts Indian immigrants in a stereotypical manner, and makes fun of them, it also serves to expose the American audience to Hindu people.

Linking Cultures

The Internet, magazines, and newspapers have contributed immensely to the spread of Hindu knowledge in America. *Hinduism Today*, for example, is a showcase for Hindu culture in America and abroad. It integrates the American Hindu and Hindu American ways. *India Abroad*, a major international newspaper, deals with all aspects of life in India and news about Indians living around the world. Both those magazines, as well as the newspapers *News India Times*, *Hindustan Times*, and *Times of India*, host popular Web sites. The interest in the American Indian community in news from "back home" is intense. The Internet has become a primary source for keeping up with events in India.

TWO IMPORTANT INDIAN FILM MAKERS

Motion pictures are enormously popular in India, and two Indian-born film makers have had a big impact in recent years on films seen by American audiences.

Writer and director M. Night Shyamalan, who was born in India in 1970, moved to the Philadelphia area with his parents shortly after his birth. He practiced Hinduism at home, but attended a Catholic school. The mixing of these two faiths and traditions—Eastern and Western—is a great source of inspiration for his work, which includes supernatural thrillers, such as *The Sixth Sense* and *Unbreakable*, both set in America. The good-vs.-evil plots also have themes of the Hindu concept of karma.

Director Mira Nair (b. 1957), on the other hand, focuses most of her work on Indian settings. She has used films such as *Salaam Bombay*, *Mississippi Masala*, and *Monsoon Wedding* to expose worldwide audiences to slices of Indian and Hindu life. Nair was born in India, but educated at Harvard. Her films have won numerous awards, including Academy Award nominations.

Sikhs living in America can turn to online sources as well, to find information about their religion, including social and political issues related to Sikh life in America. These are great sources for young American people to find out about the fun Sikh children have at their festivals. Sikhs and other people in the United States can also view videos about and hear audio quotations from the holy book, the Guru Granth Sahib, over the Internet. (Web addresses for some of these sites can be found on page 107.)

America Influences Hindus and Sikhs

We have seen how Hindu and Sikh culture and religion have influenced the American culture, but how has the American way of living affected Hindus and Sikhs in the United States? One of the major areas where Hindu life is different in America is marriage customs. There is not an easily identifiable caste system in America, and as a result, marriage traditions have been changed.

The caste system is an ancient Hindu way of dividing people into occupations. It was ruled illegal in India, but is still followed by many people there today. Traditionally, only members of the same caste could

Hindu Words and Phrases

Some popular American phrases are of Hindu origin. The phrase "what goes around, comes around" is taken from the Hindu law of karma. Karma means that what you do in this life may affect you in the next life, for good or bad. Even the term *karma* has become a familiar word for Americans. On the TV detective show *Nash Bridges*, star Don Johnson's title character once said to a captured criminal, "This is your *karma*, buddy."

The expression "Holy cow!" comes from Hindu mythology, where the cow Nandi is the sacred animal of the Hindu god Shiva. For several hundred years now, travelers to India have noticed how Hindu people regard the cow as sacred because of its ability to provide milk and butter, both major staples of life in India. To say that something is a "sacred cow" implies that it is not to be touched.

The term "Boston Brahmins" arose in the last century when that area became a hotbed of Asian philosophical thought through the influence of the Transcendentalists and the Vedanta Society. In India the Brahmins are the priests who pray to Brahma (God) and are considered to be the highest caste of people. Today, as when it was first introduced in Boston, the term denotes the first families, or the most prominent people, in society.

marry. Parents would also customarily arrange the marriage. Sometimes the marriage was arranged when the children were young and they would be married when they reached adulthood. An arranged wedding pair might not meet each other until the day of their marriage. Though this may seem odd to Americans, it has been a time-honored Hindu tradition for thousands of years.

In America, Hindus will find that they seek out the friendship of other Indian persons, not just a person of their same caste. This is because there may not be a member of one's caste in a given area. Also, Hindu and Sikh children in America have been taught about the social equality of all people. This has led some young Hindu Americans to discard the concept of caste. Many Hindu parents in America wish for their child to marry another Hindu person, especially someone who is culturally related (usually a person of Indian or Pakistani heritage). This is to preserve their religion and culture. They fear that intermarriage with a non-Hindu (or non-Sikh) or with someone of another culture may have a negative affect on the continuation of cultural and religious values.

The preservation of culture and religion are of the utmost importance to the members of the Hindu and Sikh faiths. For this reason, some Hindu and Sikh parents in America are not as concerned with the caste of the person their child marries, as long as the religion and culture are similar. There are some Hindu and Sikh parents in America, however, who believe in the caste system. They will arrange for a bride (or groom) from India to come and marry their child.

The wedding ceremony itself is the same in America as it is in India, and lasts around three to five days. In America, Hindu and Sikh marriages are conducted in homes, temples, gurdwaras, and reception halls. Some Hindus and Sikhs even travel to India for their weddings.

Young Hindus and Sikhs in America go to school and work with people who are not necessarily from their culture and/or religion. It is natural for these young people to see others in a romantic way. This presents a problem for many Hindu parents. Often, if the girlfriend or boyfriend of their child converts, or accepts the culture of the Hindu or Sikh, and wishes to teach these traditions to their own children, the parents will not take issue with the marriage. Such is the case in many instances in America. It should be noted that Sikh tradition does not believe in the same caste system that many Hindus do. However, they prefer their children to marry within the Sikh community so their religion can remain vibrant.

Between Two Worlds

As Hindus and Sikhs have increased in number in America, they have had to face challenges in many areas where their traditional culture clashes with American culture. Young people especially face this issue, often at school.

Immigrants who came to America from the Punjab and other parts of India have had to adjust to a way of life much different from the one back home. These students are faced with different expectations about what is proper behavior. They straddle two worlds. One is the traditional world of their parents and ethnic region. The other is the world of the American public school.

For instance, Hindu and Sikh children are taught to be respectful at home with their elders. Being quiet is considered being respectful. Because of this, some Hindu or Sikh children are hesitant to speak out in class. Group discussions and brainstorming types of class projects have been major adjustments for some of these students. Young women especially have had to learn to be assertive. American teachers have not always understood just why these Indian students do not participate actively in class. When grading requires class participation, these students are caught between two cultures.

Young women have other special issues. Studies have shown that it is the young women who struggle the most to adjust to life in America. What is traditionally known as "jumping into the conversation" is not a skill for them. In India, they might have attended school with only other girls and the educational system rewarded them for passive ways of learning where strict obedience to the teacher was the rule. Even those who were athletic played games only with other girls. Co-ed sports, especially the rough and tumble type, were not encouraged.

In parts of India, girls and boys do not make eye contact or engage in conversations with one another. Today, in America they may have to sit together in problem-solving group projects and attend physical education classes together. Also, many Hindu and Sikh students, male or female, are not comfortable with contact sports such as wrestling. Young women from these groups may not like wearing shorts during P.E. classes or to play on athletic teams with boys. Changing

---

ASK BEFORE YOU SHAKE

Americans take for granted that shaking hands or hugging when greeting or when parting is a friendly time honored tradition. It is not necessarily a custom endorsed by other religions and cultures. Some Hindus, traditional Sikhs, and members of Islam do not touch people who are not family members, avoiding especially contact between men and women. It is important for us to be sensitive to other belief systems. That includes personal contact with someone other than your family members.

Instead, the traditional Hindu greeting is to hold your own hands together in front of your heart and say, "Namaste," which means "I honor the divine within you."

their viewpoint about co-ed activities presents an ethical dilemma for young Hindu and Sikh immigrants.

A unique situation faced by Sikh men comes when their traditional dress clashes with a uniform required by their job. In New York Amrit Singh Rathour sued the city because as a police officer, he was forced to wear a police hat over his turban and to shave his beard. His case went to court and eventually the Equal Opportunity Commission overturned any bans on turbans and beards in the workplace. Today police officers on duty are allowed to wear their religious headgear.

American popular culture has received perhaps the greatest benefit from the ideas and styles of the Hindu and Sikh traditions. From Indian food in restaurants in every city to henna designs on junior high school girls to music heard daily on the radio, America enjoys the impact of the contributions of this vibrant and ancient culture every day.

Hindu and Sikh Impact on Society

WHILE HINDU CULTURE HAS RECENTLY BECOME MORE EVIDENT PART of American culture, the effects of Hindu Americans and their viewpoints about social issues are a bit harder to identify. Because they are a small minority in the United States, numbering about 1.5 million, it may seem as if their contributions are small. However, that is not the case. Their religious philosophy gave Americans a new knowledge of spiritual concepts. Increased acceptance by Americans of Hindu principles lets Americans borrow concepts from them in creating their own forms of spirituality.

One of the biggest issues facing Hindu culture is this level of acceptance. Just how much a part of the religious "melting pot" are they? Along with differences of faith, there are differences of culture. Indian immigrants have diverse styles of dress, may be darker in skin tone, speak with accents, or display different ways of life. All these characteristics can make it hard to mingle with Americans and people of other backgrounds. Perhaps the greatest challenge for Hindus in society is to be accepted in the communities where they live, the offices where they work, and the schools they attend. Many Hindu and Sikh organizations in America serve as centers for these community members to gather, pray, and learn. Some of the groups also play a part in reaching out to the rest of the American community.

PRECEDING PAGE
An American temple
It could be Bombay, but it is really Queens. This scene from the Hindu Temple Society of North America's large temple in that New York City borough shows how Hindu Americans have brought their culture, dress, and practices to the United States.

Self-Realization Fellowship

One of the largest organizations spreading Hindu philosophy in the United States is the Self-Realization Fellowship (SRF). The group teaches kriya yoga. H Paramahansa Yogananda (1893–1952) brought kriya yoga to the West. Before arriving in America, Yogananda founded the Yogoda Satsang Society of India in 1917.

In 1920 Yogananda came to the United States to attend a religious conference. He decided to stay. He was one of the last Hindus to get into the country before the Asian Exclusion Act was fully and finally implemented, barring the entrance of immigrants and gurus from India and elsewhere in Asia.

Americans flocked to hear Yogananda speak and a group was founded in Boston to promote his work. In 1924 he made a teaching tour that resulted in the founding of his Los Angeles headquarters in 1925. Today, there are more than 150 SRF centers or meditation groups in the United States and 180 more in 41 other countries.

He compiled his teachings in courses that could be taken at home, which made joining his movement easier. However, Yogananda was a charismatic teacher and people loved to hear him speak. He discovered the techniques of Yogoda, a system of life-energy control and spiritual development that, combined with traditional yoga, became the central concern of his teachings.

The basic practice is regular, deep meditation which leads to a direct perception of spiritual cosmic energies or the Divine. Meditating is believed to remove carbon dioxide from the blood and charge it with fresh oxygen. The invigorated atoms are then changed into currents of energy that feed the brain through the *chakras* (see chapter 3).

The unity of Eastern and Western religious teachings are also stressed by Yogananda and his philosophy. Lectures are given relating the Bible's New Testament teachings to ideas from the Bhagavad Gita, for instance. The teachings reflect the harmony and oneness between the original teachings of Jesus and those of the Hindu god Krishna.

Another belief of SRF is that there is a divine highway to God that can be taught and understood by anyone who is curious about the pathway. People can follow the principles of SRF while attending the church of your choice or heritage. This way of combining a variety of spiritual paths found popularity in America.

The Growth of Vegans

The American Vegan Society was founded by H. Jay Dinshah (1933–2000). Vegans eat only grains, vegetables, and fruits and do not eat meat or dairy products. The organization is based on the Hindu principle of *ahimsa* or "dynamic harmlessness." Veganism is a way to honor all life and to create a healthy physical and spiritual person.

The six pillars of *ahimsa* are:

• Abstinence from all animal products

• Reverence for all life

• Integrity of thought, word, and deed

• Mastery over oneself

• Service to humanity, nature, and creation

• Advancement of understanding and truth.

Such notable people as Indian civil and political rights pioneer Mahatma Gandhi and peace activist and physician Albert Schweitzer (1875–1965) were vegans. The headquarters for the society is in New Jersey, and it works with the North American Vegetarian Society and international groups. They have helped spread the spiritual and health benefits of their style of life to many Americans. Interest in "health" food has grown dramatically over recent decades in the United States. Many schools now offer vegetarian options, and restaurants of all kinds provide meatless choices to their customers. Even McDonald's has experimented with a soyburger.

Teachers Gather American Followers

Several major groups of Hindu Americans and American Hindus have come together to create communities around important teachers. This tradition of learning from a guru is very much a part of Hinduism, and American believers are not different. The groups meet together, hold events, publish articles, and books, and share their teachings with each other and the world. Here are looks at four such groups.

Chinmaya Mission West. This group is based on the work of the teacher Swami Chinmaya (1916–1993). He came to the West in the 1960s and toured the country, giving lectures and acquainting the public with

---

ONE BIG GROUP

The idea of a worldwide organization for Hindus, called a Vishwa Hindu Parisad, was first proposed in 1964. A conference was held in India in time for the great Kumbha Mela festival, and by 1970 an American branch was established in New York. Today the group based in Berlin, Connecticut, has a number of programs to serve the Hindu community.

The goals have been to provide fellowship for Hindus of different ethnic and religious groups and support programs for children. In addition to caring for Hindus, they also support festivals and the furthering of Hinduism so that members may stay connected to their heritage. In addition they help the public understand Hinduism. The group, like other Hindu groups in America, has also organized relief projects for the poor in India.

Miracle man?
Followers of Sai Baba (in robe at center) believe him to be the reincarnation of a holy man. Sai Baba founded the SAI Foundation, headquartered in California.

his methods. In 1975, he started Chinmaya Mission West and its publishing business, Chinmaya Publications West. Chinmaya's engaging personality helped gather disciples and the Mission spread rapidly. Today the American group headquarters is in Percy, California. Ashrams (places of learning), teaching centers, and missions are found throughout America and India.

The Fivefold Path. The Fivefold Path was founded in Madison, Virginia, in 1973 by Vasant Paranjipe (1918–1987), who received a divine message that he should journey to the United States and teach. The Fivefold Path is a system of yoga which begins with the purification of ones surroundings in order to engage the mind. The steps of the Fivefold Path include a fire ceremony, sharing one's assets with humility, practicing self-discipline, "doing the right thing" for your karma, and self-study. The Fivefold Path comes from the teachings of the Veda (see page 14). Vasant also blends lessons from the Bible in his teaching, helping to show that his version of Hinduism is inclusive of other beliefs.

The SAI Foundation. The SAI Foundation, based in Van Nuys, California, is the American home of a great miracle maker in India, Satya Sai Baba (born 1926). All religions have people who, many believe, can make miracles happen; Sai Baba is one such person. The first miracle of his life happened when a cobra was found underneath his bed as a child. His followers claim that this was a mysterious sign that he would develop extraordinary powers. Apparently he did, working miracles with his playmates as a child. His speciality was producing objects out of nowhere.

In 1940, he fell into a coma which lasted for two months. When he awoke he stated, "I am Sai Baba of Shirda," a popular holy man who had died in 1918. Satya Sai Baba claimed to be his incarnation. Followers say he had the ability to hold conversations with the original Sai Baba's disciples and remember what he had done in his other lifetime. People love to recount the miraculous stories of his deeds, much like followers of Jesus, Buddha, and Mohammad relate similar stories.

Interest in Sai Baba as a religious figure in America began in 1967 when he gave a set of lectures at the University of California, Santa Barbara. The California headquarters sponsors lectures, readings, and helps spread information about their leader.

Swaminarayan. This movement was brought to the United States by devotees from India in 1960s. Its founder in India was Shree Sahajanand Swami, popularly known as Swaminarayan (1781–1830). Swaminarayanan is believed to be Lord, the Supreme Being on earth and today he is still recognized as such. This group follows *bhakti,* or devotional worship that is personal, as opposed to the idea that God is impersonal. There are an estimated 60,000 devotees in the United States organized around temples in many parts of the country.

Temples as Centers of Community

Along with groups around teachers, Hindus gather together in temple groups. These groups are located in cities around the country wherever there is a large Hindu community. The temples are, of course, worship centers, and also have wide varieties of community programs for Hindus and non-Hindus. The temples serve as a way for a Hindu community to have a role and a voice in its society. Here are a few examples of major temples or temple groups.

The Hindu Temple Society of North America. Located in Flushing, New York, the temple was founded in the early 1970s to build the first Hindu temple in the United States that reflected the strict architectural standards from India. Just as there are "rules" for building Christian cathedrals or Islamic mosques, there are regular plans for Hindu temples. Temples in America that are closest in artwork to the ancient ones built in India are especially revered.

The temple in Flushing was dedicated on July 4, 1977, to honor its American home. The central shrine of the temple is dedicated to Ganesh, an elephant god known as the remover of obstacles. Whenever a Hindu takes on new responsibilities, the powers of Ganesha are invoked. Other shrines are dedicated to Shiva and his wife Parvati, and other deities.

The temple, like others in the United States raises funds for projects in India, holds community events for its members and non-members, and provides education in religion for young people. This temple and its more than 10,000 members help with senior citizen housing, and its conference center is available to the public. It also supports a medical service center and the distribution of clothing to the needy.

Devi Mandir. Devi Mandir in Napa, California, is also called the Temple of the Divine Mother. It serves both Hindu Americans and American Hindus, and its current leaders are Shree Ma and Swami Satya Nanda. Shree Ma was born in Assam, India. As a young person, Shree Ma had numerous visions and dedicated her life to religion. She heads the Santan Dharma Societies in India as well as her mission here. Nanda, on the other hand, is an American who traveled to India to seek spiritual enlightenment. He became an American Hindu who has chosen the path of devotion. When he met Shree Ma, they became inseparable and he accompanied her on celebrations of worship.

The Devi Mandir is a traditional Hindu temple where an annual round of Hindu festivals are held. In the altar area, statues of many Hindu deities are displayed, including Shiva and Saraswati. *Puja* (see page 10) is offered each day in a divine ritual. For three years at the end of the 1980s and into the 1990s Shree Ma and Nanda spent 1,000 days in the temple in continuous devotional worship.

Shiva Siddhanta Church. The Shiva Siddhanta Church was founded by master Subramuniya (born 1927), a native of California who

Big Midwest temple
Showing the growth of the Hindu community, this large, new temple near Cincinnati was dedicated in 1997 and is home to more than 18,000 Hindu devotees.

traveled to Sri Lanka. In 1949 he returned to the United States and in 1957 he founded the Subramuniya Yoga Order and opened the Christian Yoga Church, in San Francisco, to blend Western and Eastern ideas about the holy. In the late 1970s, he revised his plan and formed the Shiva Siddhanta Church.

The community life of the Shivaites is centered in temples dedicated to Shiva. The church is headed by Subramuniya's priests, who study for 12 years before taking their vows. These are vows of poverty, purity, giving up material things, obedience, and chastity.

The church is active in Hawaii and California, especially San Francisco. The church has more than 500 families as members and 5,000 students across the world, along with missions in India, Sri Lanka, and Singapore.

Hindus, Sikhs, and American Politics

FOR MANY YEARS, OFFICIAL AMERICAN POLICY MADE IT VERY difficult for Hindus and Sikhs to have any sort of political impact. Laws prohibiting immigration kept their communities small. In their early years in America, they did not have the time or energy to spend in the American political scene. Most of their time went to finding work and keeping the family together in a new country. Even as their numbers increased, they still faced the barriers of being a minority group. Their faith has also proved to be a hurdle in becoming part of society. A survey administered in August 2001 by the Hindu Leaders Forum found that 95 percent of Americans had little acquaintanceship with Hindus or Sikhs, and their religions and cultural values remain a mystery. The survey also showed that 71 percent of Americans had no contact with their Hindu neighbors. There are more than 120 Hindu temples in the United States, yet 98 percent of Americans have never been to one.

However, the Hindu community is growing in numbers and influence. Hindus in America spend some $20 billion annually on consumer goods, and some have become quite wealthy as founders of companies. Hindu and Sikh Americans also have high levels of education. Seventy-three percent are employed in the work force, a number in high-level areas of business, medicine, engineering, education, and agriculture.

Those Hindus and Sikhs who are not working in these high-paying areas often work in small businesses, such as motels, gas stations, taxis, grocery stores, and other markets. In fact, Asian-Americans of own half of the hotel rooms in America, according to figures provided by the Indian Embassy.

A Presidential Helping Hand

In the 1930s the India Welfare League and the India League of America revived efforts to obtain citizenship rights for immigrants from India. In March of 1945, President Franklin D. Roosevelt tired of the obstacles put in the way of improved immigration policies for Hindus. As Congress considered another bill to help, Roosevelt told them that he supported the bill strongly. It was not until July 1946 that Congress passed a bill granting an immigration quota to Indian nationals, allowing a small number to enter the U.S. legally each year.

At the time, India was in the middle of its long-desired break from British colonial rule. They hoped that being a democracy would improve their chances of sending more people to America. In 1949, the new Indian prime minister, Jawaharlal Nehru (1889–1964), made a major speech at the University of California at Berkeley. Nehru had worked closely with Gandhi in his movement for a free India. His speech helped open some doors for the possibility of more immigration from India to the United States. Nehru revived the hope of new political policies that would enable the old world to come to the new.

From 1965 onward, after the repeal of the Asian Exclusion Act (see page 40), the second wave of immigrants appeared. Many would be trained in high-tech fields, not as farmers or lumber workers as their ancestors had been several generations earlier. The image of Hindus would change.

A Hindu in Congress

Dalip Singh Saund worked as a farmer and merchant in California after his arrival from India in 1920. After 26 years in the United States, he finally earned American citizenship. While he was waiting out those years, he obtained three degrees from the University of California at Berkeley, including a Ph.D. in mathematics. He then settled in the older Hindu immigrant community in the Imperial Valley in central California and became an agriculturalist.

In 1956 he was elected as his district's representative to Congress, the first Indian-born member of that body and the first Hindu to hold national political office in America. Saund was a keen politician and social justice advocate who worked with civic and community groups for the betterment of all Asian peoples, including his own kinsmen, the Hindus and Sikhs. His second term in Congress was cut short by a stroke. The accomplished Saund had spent six years in the House of Representatives.

A Man of the World

New York businessman Sirdar Jagit Singh was another influential and important Sikh American. He had arrived in the United States with political experience in the 1920s, having served in the Indian National Congress. In America, he met with wealthy people in the arts who supported his import business. In the 1930s, he began to lobby unofficially for better Indian immigration and civil rights, becoming the president

Hindu political pathfinder
Dalip Singh Saund was elected to Congress in 1956, the first Hindu to serve in that body and the first Indian American as well. He represented part of the Central Valley of California.

of the newly created India League of America in 1938. This group became instrumental in drawing attention to the plight of the Hindus and Sikhs.

Singh arranged a trip to India for celebrity and socialite Claire Booth Luce, who was married to Time magazine editor Henry Luce, and later became a diplomat. Luce and Singh arranged for reporters from *Time* to talk to congressmen and politicians about the need for freedom for India. Singh's other goal was to promote immigration policies that would permit Hindus and Sikhs to come to America.

In the words of his time, Singh was a dandy dresser. He made religious, political, and ethnic fashion statements with his wardrobe, which reflected his successful participation in two worlds. He wore a black homburg hat in place of a turban and was clean-shaven when his peers wore beards. However, he continued to wear a *kara*, the thin silver bracelet that distinguished him as a Sikh.

Hands Across the Water

Relationships between Hindus in America and their relatives back in India are strong. There is so much communication between India and America that phone companies are competing to sell this community long-distance packages.

One of the reasons that Hindus in America are concerned for their family is because India has been affected by natural disasters such as earthquakes, floods, famine, and other calamities. Hindus in America are quick to respond with aid for these natural disasters, which devastate certain regions of the very large Indian subcontinent.

India-based BAPS Care International has an American home in Flushing, New York. The group held a memorial ceremony in February 2002 for victims of the 2001 earthquake that took 30,000 lives in the Indian state of Gujarat. (BAPS is an acronym for Bochasanwasi Shree Akshar Purushottam Swaminarayan Sanstha, the full name of the Indian relief group.) More than 800 people attended the event and they came from several religious groups, including Sikh, Jain, and Christian. According to the *New India Times*, Harshad Bhatt, coordinator of the event, said a group of BAPS members from India were at the scene of the earthquake in hours. Hindu Americans participated by collecting and donating money to help the victims. Dr. Dayanand Naik, a member of the American Association of Physicians of Indian Origin, said

that BAPS is building two hospitals with 45 beds each in India. In 2001, former president Bill Clinton visited several BAPS Care centers and met with the group's leaders while on a tour of India with members of the American Indian Foundation.

Particularly unsettling for Hindu Americans is the frequent outbreak of religious or political conflicts in India that put their relatives there at risk. Continuing conflict between India and neighboring Pakistan was in the news in 2002 and the world watched anxiously as those two nations threatened action against each other. Hindus in the United States were, naturally, among the most anxious. They worried about relatives back home, as well as about the possibility of war.

In response to religious and political turmoil in India, a group called the Bharatiya Vidya Bhavan USA or Institute of Indian Culture, a Jain movement, declared 2002 the Year of Nonviolence.

A feature of their celebration for peace is an essay contest for young people on "What *Ahimsa* (Nonviolence) Means to Me." For 2,600 years the Jains worked towards peace on earth. In 2002, top students with winning essays earned a trip to West Bengal and New Delhi. The goal of the program is to study the life of the local people, including education, culture, the environment, and the economy.

Flexing Political Muscle

In recent years, as the American Hindu and Indian communities have reached new levels of economic success, they have tried to put that success into action politically. Not only have their numbers as a voting group increased, their contributions to candidates and impact on positions has grown, too.

Locally, Indian-American groups have helped dozens of cities and states to make official India Day proclamations each August 15, celebrating India's freedom from Great Britain. Several Indian Americans have held local offices, including mayors in Hollywood Park, Texas; Teaneck, New Jersey; and Burien, Washington.

Nationally, groups such as the Indian American Forum for Political Education work with lawmakers to make them aware of the concerns of this growing community. The 2000 campaign for president was a coming-out party for Indian Americans in politics, especially those in Silicon Valley in California. With Indian Americans among the leaders of that community and with the encouragement of then-President Bill Clinton, they helped raise millions of dollars to support Democratic causes. Leading up to the 2000 election, Indian Americans contributed nearly $3 million to Democratic party candidates and causes, according to Dinesh Sastry, a party fundraiser.

It was not just Democrats, however, who benefited from the economic clout of the Hindu community. Republican Congressman Edward Royce of Fullerton, California, home to many Hindu and Sikh Americans, recognized that the community was trying to become more influential in national politics and made speeches to these groups in his home district.

As their numbers grow and their economic power increases, Americans from India may have an even bigger impact on politics in America in the future.

Impact of September 11

The events of September 11, 2001, had as much of an impact, or more, on the Hindu and Sikh communities as on any group in America. On that day, terrorists later found to be Islamic extremists hijacked four airplanes. They flew two into the World Trade Center in New York City and one into the Pentagon in Washington, D.C. The fourth plane crashed in Pennsylvania.

COMING TO AMERICA

Nearly 80 people per hour go to the Chennai, India, office of the U.S. Consulate applying for a visa to come to America. A new program will let them apply for an appointment with the consul over the Internet. About 300 visas are issued each day in this southern India consulate.

Following the attacks, FBI director Robert Mueller met with Hindu, Sikh, and Arab leaders in Washington, D.C., to discuss the ways some Americans behaved after that event. Mueller addressed topics such as vigilante attacks and other hate crimes. Since September 11, there have been 500 meetings among 600 organizations in an attempt to draw awareness to the distress encountered by some groups in America. Mueller said the FBI has investigated more than 300 hate crimes against minority groups and eight persons had been charged with federal offenses.

Another response was an attempt by some Hindus and Sikhs to become more involved in the political process. An example came in northern California in 2002, when Professor Sukmander Singh ran in the primary for a Congressional seat. Singh was motivated to run after dreadful attacks on his religious group after the September 11 events. Singh, who is an engineering faculty member of the University of California, Berkeley, lost the primary, but his presence in the race raised people's interest in his community and set the stage for other Hindus and Sikhs to run for political office.

HINDUS IN POLITICS

While some Hindus in America have been elected to political office, others have been named to important federal posts. For instance, the Clinton Administration employed several Hindu Americans. Some of the key officials were Dharmendra K. Sharma in the Transportation Department, Arati Prabhakar, director of the National Institute of Standards and Technology, and Preeta Bansal, a lawyer who worked in the White House.

6

Important Hindus And Sikhs in America

AS NOTED EARLIER, HINDUS OFTEN GROUP TOGETHER AROUND teachers who lead their own movements or organizations. Several such teachers are described here, as well as some of the major Hindu and Sikh groups. Other people or groups featured in this section have contributed to American life in the arts, business, and politics.

The Vedanta Society

One of the most important Hindu groups is the Vedanta Society (see page 27). It was the only permanent Hindu organization established in the United States before 1900. Sri Ramakrishna (1836–1886) was one of the founders, followed by his disciple Vivekananda. Ramakrishna attracted some followers who thought he was an *avatar*, that is, a high-level spiritual being or incarnation of a god. Vivekananda said that followers should work to help ease the suffering of humanity through social service and spiritual work.

In 1995 the society had more than 2,000 U.S. members in 13 centers, led by 14 swamis. Centers are found around the world in Argentina, France, Japan, Russia, Sri Lanka, Bangladesh and other locations. The Vedanta Society publishes *Prabuddha Bharata* or Awakened India. Local Vedanta Societies sponsor guest lectures open to people of all faiths.

Jiddu Krishnamurti (1895–1986)

Jiddu Krishnamurti (see also page 27) was groomed as a young child by Theosophists to be the next world savior. He renounced that claim and went on to become a more than successful independent teacher. The Krishnamurti Foundation of America was founded in 1969 to spread his teachings.

Krishnamurti was born into a high-caste Brahmin family on May 12, 1895, in Andhra Pradesh, India. Until his death in 1986 he was a gifted and unusual teacher. He said his mission was to set people free from dogma or doctrine, including his own. He believed that humans had to be their own guru and attracted well-educated people who desired the freedom he talked about. Krishnamurti believed that until people were free from fear and manipulation by authority figures, they would continue to harm others in their misguided way and humanity would continue to suffer.

He taught that education could be used as a tool to help integrate the mind and heart. This education, he believed, would enable students overcome the social forces that affect their thinking. He established many schools in the United States, Great Britain, and India. The Krishnamurti Foundation of America works with other organizations around the world and houses a library with material from Krishnamurti's talks. It also runs Oak Grove, a school in Ojai, California.

Maharishi Mahesh Yogi (b. 1918)

The group founded by Maharishi teaches a meditation technique called transcendental meditation (TM). It has played a big role in the history of Hinduism in America and Western societies. Guru Dev rediscovered this ancient method of meditation in India and passed it on to Maharishi, who spent 13 years in seclusion with Guru Dev learning about his teachings.

After Guru Dev's death, Maharishi came forward in 1957 to tell the world about TM. His movement grew slowly until some celebrities became students. The Beatles and actresses Mia Farrow and Jane Fonda all practiced the method; others followed them. Maharishi established the World Plan for TM, with 3,600 centers worldwide. Through the teaching of TM, he believed, the Age of Enlightenment would begin. TM is taught at colleges through the Student International Meditation Society, and the Maharishi International University is near Fairfield, Iowa.

The essence of TM is a form of personal meditation using a mantra as a repetitive sound. Individuals are given their own secret mantra that is supposed to work for them. They also offer prayers to Hindu deities.

For a time the group denied the religious components of its organization in an attempt to be declared a non-religious group. The group's leaders thought these teachings would be more easily accepted if spread this way. The U.S. government decided the organization was indeed religious and some of its programs, such as teaching TM in public schools, were halted. By 1984 more than 1 million people had taken a course in TM. Today, many people who follow other religious paths still enjoy and practice TM in their lives.

Man of many talents
A teacher, writer, musician, and peace activist, Sri Chinmoy also has helped his followers achieve success in athletic feats of endurance, such as 100-mile runs.

Sri Chinmoy (b. 1931)

Sri Chinmoy Kumar Ghose was born in India in 1931. At 12 years old he entered the ashram of Sri Aurobindo and endured intense spiritual discipline. An inner command told him to come to the West in 1964 to be of service to spiritual seekers here. Sri Chinmoy teaches a path of yoga that directs the practitioner to union with God. His path calls for discipline, including meditation, vegetarianism, and celibacy. Sri Chinmoy accepts all religions, charges no fees to study his path, and has the utmost devotion for Christ, Buddha, Krishna, and other religious figures of the world.

He encourages athletic activities and sponsors relay runs for world peace. Some of the people who follow him have accomplished some amazing physical feats, such as long-distance endurance running or doing somersaults for many miles. Sri Chinmoy himself is a prolific author, composer, and artist. He has written more than 1,300 books of poetry and essays, and he has composed 13,000 devotional songs (*bhakti*) in English and his native Bengali. He has drawn more than 4 million "soul birds," pictures of the human spirit in the form of a bird.

Often described as an ambassador of peace, he has offered free concerts and mediation groups to fund world peace and has conferred with world leaders about how to achieve peace on a troubled planet. Authorities around the world have dedicated natural wonders such as rivers, lakes, gardens, and waterfalls to him.

Baba Ram Dass (b. 1931)

The Hanuman Foundation in Santa Fe, New Mexico, blends a variety of traditional Hindu ideas for Americans. The Foundation was started in 1974 by Baba Ram Dass, who was born Richard Alpert. He was asked to leave Harvard along with a colleague, Timothy Leary, because of their experiments with LSD, a now-illegal drug. Alpert became interested in using meditation to reach enlightenment and sought the teachings of a guru. He traveled to India in 1967 to meet Guru Maharaji.

Maharaji taught Richard Alpert a type of yoga and meditation. Alpert felt himself become a different person, and changed his name to Ram Dass. (It is not unusual to change one's name when adopting a different religious path.) While in study with the Maharaji, Ram Dass also developed a liking for Hanuman, the loveable, monkey-faced deity of Hinduism.

Upon returning to the west, Baba Ram Dass wrote and published *Be Here Now* (published in 1971) which emphasized his ideal of living in the present moment, rather than being tied to the past or yearning for the future. Dass taught that all people are on a journey to Enlightenment. He also taught that no one would be left out, there would be a teacher for everyone.

A temple built by Dass and his followers is located in Taos, New Mexico. It houses a 1,500-pound marble statue of Hanuman that Dass had made and imported from India. The temple serves more than 300 families from Albuquerque to Denver. There are weekly and yearly festivals and services.

Alice Coltrane (b. 1937)

The Vedantic Center in Agoura, California, was founded in 1975 in Los Angeles by Alice Coltrane. Raised in Detroit, Coltrane dedicated the early years of her career to performing as a jazz musician, as had her late husband, John Coltrane. When Alice turned 31, she left the music business and entered a period of spiritual isolation. When it was over she had revolutionized her life and become a swami. She soon organized the Vedantic Center in Los Angeles.

Coltrane wrote several books and her group bought land in rural southern California to establish Sai Anatman Ashram for its members. The Vedantic Center there is unique because it is one of the very few Hindu organizations drawing members predominantly from the African-American community. There are many ashrams and centers throughout the United States with black members, but Coltrane's center is unique in being led by a woman serving a largely black ashram.

Joyce Green (b. 1940)

Joyce Green was born into a working class family in Brooklyn, New York. She lost her mother when 13 years old. Her first human rights teachers were four homeless black people she met living under the boardwalk at Coney Island. It was from friendships formed with them that she learned, "There are no throwaway people."

A mother of three, married, and living in the suburbs, her life—once quite ordinary—unfolded in a spectacular way. In an attempt to lose weight, she went to the gym and enrolled in a yoga class. Learning new ways to breathe (*prana*) helped her to lose weight. Much to her surprise, more than her weight began to change. Through her new breathing patterns she experienced visions while in ecstatic trance. Over the following years, she spiritually evolved into Ma Jaya Sati Bhagavati, known simply as Ma. She started The Kashi Foundation, an organization with medical, educational, and spiritual projects around the world.

In 1976, Ma and her students moved to Florida and established the Neem Karoli Baba Kashi Ashram, a multi-religious community committed to helping and teaching others. Ma helps the poor and the sick who cannot take care of themselves. She is united with other major spiritual leaders in gaining awareness of the plight of innocent children, women, and men who are victimized. One of Ma's religious principles is that all religious paths lead home to God. In Hinduism, this means devotional prayer (*bhakti*), yogas, karma, and meditation.

One of the most unique projects Ma and her group started was the Ma Jaya River School in Florida, for children of all faiths and ethnic

IN A TRANCE

When someone is in an ecstatic trance, they are no longer in touch with the everyday world. Some believe that a person in such a state is experiencing a reality much different from the everyday world. People who experience these mystical states can be of any religion or ethnic group. Every religious group has mystics who achieve very high states of consciousness. Some people have made fun of mystics and thought them very odd because these trances can not be explained in a scientific manner. Scientists and religious people are working to provide new models of understanding that will explain this behavior. Even people who do not consider themselves religious have reported them.

A different path
New York homemaker and
mother Joyce Green became
the important American
Hindu teacher and commu-
nity leader Ma Jaya. Her
groups work in education
and in taking care of people
suffering from disease.

groups. It is a private school that emphasizes both academics and spirituality in an environment of love, caring, and non-judgment. The school
combines service to others, such as helping at Mary's House, a home
for babies with AIDS, and other facilities. Through their Service Learning Program, the River School serves 1,200 people in nursing homes,
hospitals, and assisted living facilities. More than 10,000 people a year
are touched by these students, who have learned that service to humanity is a celebration of human compassion. The programs at River
House also include college prep classes, problem-solving, creative arts,
and more.

Vidya Dehejia (b. 1942)

Professor Vidja Dehejia, a former teacher and curator of Asian art at Columbia University, has built the Asian Collection at the Smithsonian National Museum into a remarkable display of Indian artifacts, paintings and sculpture. Dehejia was the only South Asian American to be listed in the December 2001 issue of *Washingtonian* magazine as one of the 50 brightest and best world class Washingtonians.

How did she become the highest ranking Hindu American to run a national museum of art? She said her father used to drive her family to ancient monuments and sites of creative art in India and she became enthralled. Hopefully, her work will let more people know that South Asian culture can stand side by side with other ancient or contemporary cultures in its unique artistic splendor.

Vinod Kholsa (b. 1955)

Indian Americans were at the heart of the technology revolution that swept through America and the world in the 1990s. One of the most prominent investors and executives was Vinod Kholsa. As a young man in his native India, he knew early on that he wanted to be a success in the business world.

After studying business in India, Kholsa came to America in 1976 to attend college. After graduating from Stanford Business School, he helped start several technology companies in California, one of which was Sun Microsystems, which soon became one of the largest computer companies in the world. Kholsa was eventually chairman and chief executive officer.

After leaving Sun a wealthy man, he became a venture capitalist, which is an investor who helps start other companies. In the computer newspaper *The Industry Standard,* writer Vishesh Kumar said (in an article called "Vinod Kholsa Still Believes" in February 2001), "Kholsa is the closest thing there is in the venture capital world to a superstar. He makes zillions of dollars in the venture funds run by Kleiner Perkins Caufield & Byers," with whom Kholsa works. He was very influential in helping several young companies get funding to start, and remains a prominent player in Silicon Valley.

Other important Hindu American business leaders include Desh Despande of Sycamore Networks, Sanjiv Sidhu of i2 Technologies, and Rakesh Gangwal of US Airways.

Other Hindu and Sikh Contributions

The U.S. Congressional Caucus on India and Indian Americans, founded in 1993 by Reps. Frank Pallone and Bill McCollum, is one way that Indian American leaders are recognized. The Caucus works with Indian national agencies to spread the word.

"The contributions of Asian Indians has been outstanding," wrote Devendra Singh, minister for community affairs, at the Indian Embassy in Washington, in a May 2002 press release. "The Hindu Americans have been role models for immigrants who come to this country."

Singh noted that Har Gobind Khorana of the Massachusetts Institute of Technology had been awarded the prestigious 1968 Nobel Prize in medicine.

Singh added that Subramanyam Chandrashekar of the University of Chicago was recognized by several professional organizations for his innovative research in physics. These and other notables demonstrate that the impact of Hindu immigration on America has been a positive one.

Singh also noted that a key element in the success of these individuals is their belief in family values and education. Parents played a sound role in giving their children the focus that education, as well as being a good persons.

Sikh Coalition

For several years now, there have been groups aimed at organizing the Sikh communities around the United States. In the aftermath of September 11, 2001, these groups suddenly were thrust into prominence. One such group is the Sikh Coalition, which is based in New York City.

The Sikh Coalition works with national and local governments to ensure equal rights for Sikhs and to fight against discrimination. The misplaced anger toward Sikhs following the attacks of September 11, 2001, was a call to action for this group. It aggressively tracked hate crimes against Sikhs, while also working closely with the media to provide accurate information about Sikhs and Sikh traditions. Its Web site reports on all mentions of Sikhs in the media, whether positive or negative, and gathers information for use in its own publicity.

The group works with other cultural and ethnic groups to promote racial harmony and equal rights, and also provides assistance for Sikhs in need.

7

Hindus and Sikhs: Today and Tomorrow

WE HAVE LOOKED AT HINDU AND SIKH TRADITIONS AS A RELIGION, AS well as a culture, and seen what these groups have experienced in America. The areas of social policy, political challenges, and cultural contributions dominate their struggle to become part of the nation. Knowing that, what can we say about how these religions will continue to develop in America?

Immigrants, as we have read earlier, brought Hinduism to America from the Indian subcontinent more than 100 years ago. Some Hindus also came to the United States from countries such as Trinidad or South Africa. As long as Hindu immigrants continue to come here, there will always be a new infusion of Hinduism.

However they got here, the children of Hindu and Sikh immigrants and their descendants will, if they stay together as an ethnic and religious group, most likely carry on the traditions of their parents and grandparents. Although the tradition may be somewhat different than the way it is practiced in India, certain aspects of the Hindu and Sikh faiths will live on with future generations of Hindus and Sikhs in America. Studies have shown that when new immigrants arrive in the United States, they remain together for several generations, and then begin to marry into other groups. When this happens, the heritage changes.

Working to Stay Together

Hindu Americans are struggling to hold their traditions together. Most want their children to marry other Hindus. An arranged marriage is a way of life that has origins in India but continues here. Arranged marriages are more stable and have a lower divorce rate than love marriages. At the heart of Hindu culture is the sanctity of the family. Parents and children are particularly close and the grandparents are revered for their contributions to family life. It is not unusual to find three generations of a family sharing the same home, where children are always cared for by a family member. Even when living in separate homes, Hindu and Sikh Americans maintain close contact with each other. It is rare for them to place their elderly family members in assisted living facilities or nursing homes. They believe that the elderly should be taken care of by their children so that the circle of family love and respect is unbroken.

The very nature of Hinduism allows for flexibility in religious belief and practice. There is no rigid dogma, or set of lessons, that requires each Hindu to practice their faith in a certain prescribed manner. It is a matter of personal and individual choice. Hinduism can flourish in modern America while still retaining its essential core. New studies show that when Hindu and Sikh Americans return to India, it is primarily to visit family and religious sites.

Today, the temples and gurdwaras in America are gathering places. American society often seems to value the non-holy or "earthly" more than the sacred; this can be a challenge for Hindus in America. However, Hindu and Sikh Americans are in the forefront of preserving a religion and culture that they consider too important to abandon.

Hinduism over the centuries has adapted in many different ways that fit the local time and place. This ability allows the Hindu faithful to participate in any social setting while still retaining their Hindu faith, beliefs, and practices. They join the society they live in, but pass down the traditions of their faith within their families. As time goes by, however, Hindus will intermarry with non-Hindus, and Hinduism will probably change.

One of the results of Hindu immigration to the United States is the movement away from the caste system. It is being replaced with the democratic idea of Hindus as one people. In the United States, being a Hindu has become more important than being of a certain caste or

PRECEDING PAGE
A marriage in Queens
This photo of a Hindu wedding ceremony was taken in 2001 in New York City, at the Hindu Temple Society of North America in the borough of Queens. However, the traditions, dress, music, and ceremonies were just as they would have been in India.

Wave the flag for Sikhs
*This young Sikh is taking
part in a parade in New York
celebrating the 300 years
of the organization Khalsa
(see page 23).*

class. Similar to other groups in American history, Hindus have felt
comfortable sticking together because of their minority status in the
United States. All castes and sects of Hindus in America have faced
some cultural, economic, or social discrimination, whether due to their
faith or their ethnicity. In this shared sense of isolation, Hindus and
Sikhs find solace with each other and within their own communities.

Kumar's Story, Continued

(See page 30 for more from Kumar.)

In college in Florida I studied microbiology, but also began to take many religious studies courses. My experiences in high school, my upbringing, and my international travels led me to desire a greater knowledge of the religious traditions of the world. I enjoyed doing all the reports and essays in my religion classes. I loved reading about Hinduism, Sikhism, Buddhism, Christianity, and other world religions. I loved history and learning languages. I loved doing research on religious groups and learning what people believed, why they believed those things, and how various religious groups have changed over the years. In fact, some of the information I gathered is right here in a few of the chapters of this book.

As I did all this at college, I rediscovered my Indian and Hindu heritage. I also met a number of Hindus and Sikhs at the university. There were also a lot of students at the university from India who were new to the United States. They would often (and still do) come up to meet me and say something like "Namaste bhaisaab," which means "Hello, fellow brother." They came to me because they recognized a familiar Indian face in a new country. I started to realize that Hindus and Sikhs from India really feel lonely when they come to America. They love the educational activities, but miss their homeland. Through my studies, I wanted to make sure that I did not lose my cultural and religious identity like a lot of other people in America.

Having a shared heritage give them an identity while developing a new life in America. Sponsoring parades, rallies, and festivals, for example, celebrate their traditions while also inviting the general public to join them, much as Irish immigrants used St. Patrick's Day parades and festivities to help them become part of the American social fabric.

Battling Public Perceptions

One major obstacle to the continued growth of Hinduism in America is the lack of mainstream attention. Unless a person buys a book about the Sikh or Hindu tradition, visits a temple, or takes a religious studies class at a university, or happens to meet a Hindu or Sikh person, there is not much in everyday life with information about Hinduism. In fact, rather than presenting relevant information about Hindus and Sikhs, some commentators have even attacked them for their beliefs. For instance, television preacher Pat Robertson, host of the Christian Broadcasting Network talk show called *The 700 Club*, portrays Hinduism as evil and demonic.

By accusing Hinduism of being demonic, Robertson is perpetuating an old stereotype. Some conservative Christians feel that the Hindu concept of many manifestations of divine forms (gods and goddesses) is not right. They expand this belief into thinking that because Hinduism differs from Christianity in the ways that it does, that it is evil. In addition, this viewpoint of Hindu and Sikh faith offers justification to those seeking to evangelize (convert to Christianity) Hindus and Sikhs. However, religious studies experts feel that to try to apply Christian concepts to Hindu ideas is like comparing apples to oranges. The two systems are too different to compare in such direct ways.

Optimistic Outlooks

Despite these obstacles, Hinduism is experiencing more and more acceptance in America. Non-Indian Americans are becoming interested in Hinduism mainly through colleges and universities that offer classes on Hinduism and Indian culture. Members of the American mainstream are integrating Hindu ideas (like karma and dharma) into their thinking. The continuing growth of yoga as a physical activity opens many people's eyes to Hindu principles, not as a rival to their own faith and beliefs, but as another way to experience spirituality.

Hindus in America are becoming more community-oriented and every year new Hindu temples are established. With the continued growth of these temples and the Hindu American communities that surround them, the American community at large is becoming more conscious of Hinduism and of people who have ancestral roots in India. Hindu temples and Sikh gurdwaras serve, in a way, as announcements for Indian culture in America.

More people are becoming educated about Hinduism by reading about it. Students are usually the first members of their family to research Hinduism when they are assigned a book report. American students are generally encouraged to learn about diverse cultures and religions. This educational focus, based on the concepts of freedom of speech and religion, fosters the openness that is required to understand the religions of others.

How Hinduism and Sikhism Have Survived

Hindus in America have sometimes been criticized for adapting their faith to this culture. Adapting has been the key to keeping Hinduism alive. By forming a synthesis (a blend) with different faiths and cultures, Hinduism survived rival ideas by incorporating them. As Hinduism adapts, it allows its followers freedom to practice Hinduism in any manner they choose. This appeals to people of many cultural and religious backgrounds.

However, while some adaptation can make the faith live on, preservation of the core beliefs and practices is essential for the survival of the faiths in America. Parents are attempting to keep their language skills current so that their children will learn the languages of the religion (many religious songs and rituals are not in English). They provide a role model for their children to follow, preserving and observing the rituals that they want to pass down to their children, while also having their children participate when possible. Thus, although these rituals may be adapted for American life, and occasionally it can be a struggle to keep them as part of a family's life, they are not abandoned completely.

Studies have shown that Hindu and Sikh parents who instill religious values in their children find that those children grow up to adopt those values as their own, and teach them to their own children. For example, although Hindu young people in America are more free to choose their own spouses, a commitment to traditional values is often taken into consideration when making this choice.

As has been shown throughout the century that Hindu and Sikh culture have been part of America, American culture can change the settings, the forms, or the styles of Hindu and Sikh practice within families and within communities, but beneath these adaptations is a solid foundation of tradition and faith.

The Question of Intermarriage

Aside from parental support, marriage is the second major factor affecting the future of the Hindu and Sikh traditions in America. As mentioned earlier, many traditional families wish their children to marry Hindus or Sikhs. As Hindu and Sikh children grow up in America, chances are that there will be a great number of them who fall in love with people from other cultures and religions. This presents a great dilemma for both the parents and the child.

Some spouses will convert to the religion to preserve the family's heritage. Some families will ask the non-native spouse to learn the language. Some will ask that the children from the resulting marriage be brought up in the full Hindu or Sikh tradition. Still, some families will be happy if the spouse embraces the culture, if not the religion. There are a number of Hindu and Sikh families who are very content with the marital choices of their sons and daughters, and do not have problems with intermarriage. In contrast, there are some parents who will never accept intermarriage. Many Hindu and Sikh youth in this country, and their families here and abroad, are faced with this issue.

Reflections

The Hindu and Sikh traditions have been an integral and growing part of recent American history. They have been involved in social issues, political scenes, culture, and every other aspect of our society. It is exciting to watch the evolution of the Hindu and Sikh traditions in the United States. These traditions, however, are changing in America. With the continued immigration from India and other countries, a majority of Hindu and Sikh families are still relatively new to this country. Only time will tell how future generations of Hindus and Sikhs will continue to enrich the cultural and religious landscape of America.

GLOSSARY

ahimsa Nonviolence to living creatures. Practiced in the Jain, Hindu, and Buddhist traditions, and source of inspiration for Gandhi in his non-violent Indian independence movement.

ashram Place of meditation, usually for priests or religious people. Some followers may live in an ashram as well.

atman The name of the soul in Hindu thought.

avatar Important gods that come to earth to teach people. These include such gods as Vishnu and Krishna.

baba A term of honor, endearment, or devotion. A person of great holiness is called a *babaji*.

Bhagavad Gita The sixth book of the great epic Mahabharata where Krishna teaches Arjuna about self duty and devotion.

bhakti The devotional path to god through loving service.

bhajan A Hindu devotional song.

chela Hindi word for student.

darshan The seeing of the divine image.

dharma Proper behavior, cosmic duty, and responsibility.

Gayatri The most common prayer in Hinduism to Savitar, the sun god.

gurdwara Temple and meeting place for followers of the Sikh tradition.

Guru A teacher or spiritual guide.

kach Special part of Sikh dress; short pants designed to facilitate quick movement. One of the "five Ks."

kara A steel bracelet signifying restraint, worn by men of the Sikh tradition. One of the "five Ks."

kangh Traditional Sikh comb. One of the "five Ks."

kesh Word meaning to grow the hair long, which Sikh men do as a sign of saintliness. One of the "five Ks."

kirpan Short dagger carried by Sikh men as one of the "five Ks."

kirtan The singing of hymns as a form of worship.

Khalsa The world *khalsa* means pure. It is the name for a fellowship of Sikhs founded by Sobind Singh in 1699.

mahatma A title given to a person of great wisdom.

maya The idea that believing this world is permanent is really an illusion.

mandala The colorful sacred art work that leads one to a focal point with God.

mantra A sacred word or verse that is chanted regularly, such as "om."

mandir The sacred Hindu temple.

moksa Release from the bonds of the earth.

monism The idea that all of life is one unified reality.

monotheism The idea that there is one God who is separate and apart from the world.

murti Paintings or pictures that depict gods or goddesses.

polytheism The worshiping of more than one deity.

puja The worship ceremony to a deity where one offers flowers, food and incense as a measure of respect and devotion to that God.

Ram An avatar of Vishnu. A major player in the epic literature the Ramayana.

rishi A revered religious sage or wise man.

sadhu A person who has experienced God through meditation.

samsara The endless round of birth and rebirth.

sannyasin One who has renounced the care of the world in search of God.

shakti The divine female energy usually dramatized as a goddess.

shruti Scripture stories that are recited or heard, as opposed to being written down.

Singh The name taken by male Sikhs. This is also the last name of some Hindus who are not Sikhs.

smirti Scripture that is remembered or memorized, as opposed to being heard or written.

swami A teacher of religious principles.

Tirtha The ford where several rivers flow together. Believed to be sacred grounds by the Hindu, Sikh, Jain, and other traditions.

Upanishads The sacred collection of teachings about humans and God that were passed down from the teacher, guru to the student chela over the centuries.

Vedas The oldest sacred scripture of the Hindus. The Upanishads are the last of the Vedas

yoga Techniques of spiritual discipline. Some emphasize breathing and movements that teach one how to get out of a world of suffering and achieve enlightenment.

yogi A person who practices yoga in an attempt to reach *moksa*.

TIME LINE

1825	Ram Mohan Roy's book, *The Precepts of Jesus*, brought to America.
1883	Protap Mazoomdar visits the home of Mrs. Ralph Waldo Emerson in Massachusetts.
1886	Emma Curtis Hopkins helps found the New Thought movement, partly inspired by Hindu teachings.
1893	Parliament of Religions is held in Chicago
	Virchand Gandhi, first Jain to visit America, arrives for Parliament.
1903	First Sikhs to emigrate to Canada arrive.
	First U.S. Sikh gurdwara built in Stockton, California.
	Alien Land Law passes, preventing non-citizens from owning land or property.
1917	Asian Exclusion Act passes, severely limiting immigration from India and Asia.
1920s	Jiddu Krishnamurti begins visits to America.
	Yogananda arrives, later to found Self-Realization Fellowship.
	Supreme Court rules against Indian (non-white) citizenship in *United States vs. Bhagat Singh Thind*.
	Immigration rules eased slightly by Congress.
1948	India achieves independence from Great Britain; independence leader Mahatma Gandhi is assassinated.
1956	Dalip Saund Singh becomes first Indian American elected to Congress, representing central California.
1965	Asian Exclusion Act is repealed, paving the way for increased immigration of Hindus and Sikhs from India, as well as members of other faiths from Asian countries.
	Swami Prabhupada comes to America to establish ISKCON there.
1971	*Be Here Now*, a book by Ram Dass, is published.
	Bhagwan Shree Rajneesh arrives in America.
2001	After terrorist attacks, many Sikhs are targets of violence and discrimination as misguided people believe them to be connected to Islam.

RESOURCES

Reading List

Clarke, Peter, ed., *The World's Religions*. Pleasantville, N.Y.: Reader's Digest, 1993.

Dubois, Abbe, *Hindu Manners, Customs, and Ceremonies*. New Delhi: Rupa and Co., 1999.

Ganeri, Anita, *What Do We Know About Hinduism?* New York: Peter Bedrick Books, 1996.

Johnsen, Linda, *The Complete Idiot's Guide to Hinduism*. Indianapolis, Ind.: Alpha Books, 2002.

Melton, J. Gordon, ed., *American Religious Creeds. Vol. 3*. New York: Triumph Books, 1991.

―――――――, *Encyclopedia of American Religions, 5th ed*. Detroit: Gale Press, 2000.

―――――――, *Religious Leaders of America*, 2nd ed. Detroit: The Gale Group.1999.

Molloy, Michael, *Experiencing the World's Religions*. Calif.: Mayfield Publishing Co., 1999.

Olivelle, Patrick, *The Panchatantra: The Book of India's Folk Wisdom*. New York: Oxford University Press.1997.

Singh, Nikky-Guninder Kaur, *Sikhism (World Religions Series)*, rev. ed. New York: Facts On File, 1993.

Wangfu, Madhu Bazaz, *Hinduism (World Religions Series),* rev. ed. New York: Facts On File, 2001.

Williams, Raymond Brady, *Religions of Immigrants from India and Pakistan*. New York: Cambridge University Press. 1988.

Resources on the Web

Hindu Temple Society of North America
www.nyganeshtemple.org
Home site of the largest Hindu temple group in the West, located in Queens, New York. Details about temple events and background on Hinduism.

Hindu Resources Online
www.hindu.org
A clearinghouse for Web sites and other information sources about Hinduism.

Sikh Coalition
www.sikhcoalition.org
A support and information group for Sikhs in North America, focusing on providing accurate information for the media.

SikhNet Youth Forum
www.sikhnet.com/s/Youth+And+Children
Games, stories, and tales for Sikh children.

Vedanta Society
www.vedanta-newyork.org (New York chapter)
www.vedanta.org (Southern California chapter)
Two sites that feature information about one of the oldest Hindu organizations in the United States.

INDEX

Note: *Italic* page numbers refer to illustrations.